CROCHET HOME

CROCHET HOME

20 VINTAGE MODERN CROCHET
PROJECTS FOR THE HOME

EMMA LAMB

David and Charles

www.stitchcraftcreate.co.uk

CONTENTS

WELCOME TO MY CROCHET HOME!

Here you will find perfectly pretty pillows, fabulous granny-chic inspired potholders, beautiful blankets and throws and delightful decorations to crochet. I have included some of my most popular designs to date, such as the Tiny Squares Patchwork Cushion, as well as my original flower garland and circular floor throw, both re-invented especially for this book – take a peek at the colourful Scarborough Rock Floor Throw and Flower Garlands. Sprinkled between these signature pieces are a few new gems, including my favourites, the Day Dreamer Dreamcatcher and the epic, stash-busting Granny Chic Pinwheel Blanket.

For each project I have worked tirelessly to source the most perfect yarn, chosen either because of its beautiful, unique quality or because of its vast range of colours – you'll find that some amazing fibres have been used such as wool, linen, paper, alpaca and organic cotton, and sometimes you will have the whole spectrum to choose from.

I hope you have fun discovering new yarns, enjoying a healthy dose of colour and creating beautiful objects for your home. Happy crocheting!

Emma

GETTING STARTED

CHARTS

All twenty patterns in this book are written using UK crochet terms, and each design includes the relevant crochet charts to complete the project.

These charts use the standard universal crochet symbols; there is a full list of these symbols, including both UK and US terminology, to familiarize yourself with before diving headlong into the patterns (see **Pattern Abbreviations and Symbols**).

If you are unfamiliar with any of the stitches used, refer to the handy **Techniques** section, which includes a step-by-step guide for each type of stitch.

Crochet charts read exactly as a piece of crochet is created. Motifs worked in the round start at the centre, beginning with the foundation chain or adjustable ring, and are read anticlockwise, just as they are crocheted, with the start of each new round being numbered accordingly. Generally, motifs worked in rows begin at the bottom or bottom left corner with a foundation chain; odd numbered rows are then worked from right to left and even numbered rows are worked left to right. One more thing to note: the crochet charts do not include information on colour placement; for this, please refer to the written pattern or any diagrams provided.

TENSION

The patterns also include information on tension (gauge) and the type of tension swatch you will need to work before you begin your project. In most cases it will be a blocked version of one of these three samples:

– a standard granny square motif worked in three treble shells of up to eight rounds, depending on the weight of yarn being used

– a simple circular motif worked in treble stitches with a twelve stitch increase in each round, up to eight rounds as before

– a square swatch with rows of treble stitches built from a foundation chain

Take note of how each finished project should be blocked and use this method for blocking your tension swatch (see Blocking). Measure your stitch count over a 10cm (4in) grid to see if it matches the required tension. If it does, you can get started on your lovely project. However, if you have too many stitches you will need to go up a hook size, and if you have too few you will need to go down a hook size. You may need to experiment a little with hook sizes until you get the tension right, but this is an essential part of any project. If you do not match your tension accurately your project may not come out at the right size, or worse you may end up running out of yarn!

Checking your tension carefully is especially useful when substituting the recommended yarn with your own favourite. Once you have accurately matched your tension you will then need to cross reference the meterage of the recommended yarn with your substitute to determine how much you will need to complete your project. Each pattern already includes a reasonable allowance so you should aim to match the quantity of the stated yarn as closely as possible.

BLOCKING

Most of the projects in this book require steam blocking or pressing. This is my preferred method for blocking crochet as it is quick, easy and less likely to distort the finished piece than using the wet-blocking process. Crochet fabric is much denser than knitted fabric, using up to a third more yarn than knitting, so it will hold more water than knitted fabric during the wet-blocking process, making it heavier and more prone to stretching or distorting in ways it shouldn't.

To steam block you will need both a steam iron and a press cloth. A press cloth can be a simple sheet of fine cotton, or any heat-proof fabric that will allow steam to pass through it while protecting your projects from accidental scorching. Small projects can be easily blocked on an ironing board but for a large blanket you will obviously need a larger surface, such as a floor. To protect your floor lay out old blankets or sheets to a size larger than your project (vintage wool blankets are ideal here), then lay your project on top smoothing out any creases. For circular and lap blankets, start at the centre and work outward gently adjusting as you go until the final shape lies neatly, and using a tape measure to ensure even proportions. For larger blankets, it is best to start at a corner and fan out from there.

PATTERN ABBREVIATIONS & SYMBOLS

GENERAL ABBREVIATIONS

UK crochet terms are used throughout the written project patterns; please be aware that these differ slightly from US stitch terms. The crochet charts, however, use standard stitch symbols and both UK and US translations are included here for ease of reference. Note that US stitches are referenced [in brackets] in the **Techniques** section.

st(s)	stitch(es)	rnd	round
ch-sp(s)	chain space(s)	inc	increase
sp	space	dec	decrease
rep	repeat	RS	right side
prev	previous	WS	wrong side

Chart Symbol	UK	Description	US	Description
ꕷ		adjustable ring (or magic loop)		adjustable ring (or magic loop)
►		starting point		starting point
○	ch	chain	ch	chain
•	ss	slip stitch	ss	slip stitch
+	dc	double crochet	sc	single crochet
T	htr	half treble	hdc	half double crochet
⊺	tr	treble	dc	double crochet
⊧	dtr	double treble	tr	treble
⋎	2dc inc	increase by working two double crochet stitches into the same space	2sc inc	increase by working two single crochet stitches into the same space
V	2tr inc	increase by working two treble stitches into the same space	2dc inc	increase by working two double crochet stitches into the same space
Ⅷ	3tr shell	work three treble stitches into the same space	3dc shell	work three double crochet stitches into the same space
⋀	tr2tog	decrease two treble stitches together	dc2tog	decrease two double crochet stitches together
⋔	tr3tog	decrease three treble stitches together	dc3tog	decrease three double crochet stitches together

Chart Symbol	UK	Description	US	Description
	tr4tog	decrease four treble stitches together	dc4tog	decrease four double crochet stitches together
	dtr2tog	decrease two double treble stitches together	tr2tog	decrease two treble stitches together
	3tr-cl	three treble cluster	3dc-cl	three double crochet cluster
	4tr-cl	four treble cluster	4dc-cl	four double crochet cluster
	2dtr-cl	two double treble cluster	2tr-cl	two treble cluster
	3dtr-cl	three double treble cluster	3tr-cl	three treble cluster
	5tr-fpcl	five treble front post cluster	5dc-fpcl	five double crochet front post cluster
	pc	popcorn stitch including chain finish	pc	popcorn stitch including chain finish
	pc	popcorn stitch excluding chain finish	pc	popcorn stitch excluding chain finish
	sdc	spike double crochet	ssc	spike single crochet
	bp-htr	back post half treble	bp-hdc	back post half double crochet
	s-tr	starting treble (no chains)	s-dc	starting double crochet (no chains)
	f2tr inc	foundation two treble increase	f2dc inc	foundation two double crochet increase
–	jn	joining stitch	jn	joining stitch
+	jdc	joining double crochet	jsc	joining single crochet
●	pf	place fabric snippet	pf	place fabric snippet
- - - -		invisible fasten off		invisible fasten off
*		hand stitching		hand stitching

REPEATS WITHIN PATTERNS

When following repeated pattern instructions, note that the repeats marked with asterisks denote the total number of repeats.

FLOWER GARLANDS

Some crocheters find the humble granny square to be their crochet therapy, but for me it's flowers – in all colours, sizes and shapes. It is my opinion that an hour spent with a crochet hook and gorgeous floral-coloured yarn making a pile of pretty petals is an hour spent very wisely indeed. I have designed three pretty floral motifs and two sizes of leaf for this garland. The pattern instructions describe one possible arrangement for stringing them together, but with a little imagination they can be combined in dozens of different ways with almost endless colour combinations. Let your imagination run free!

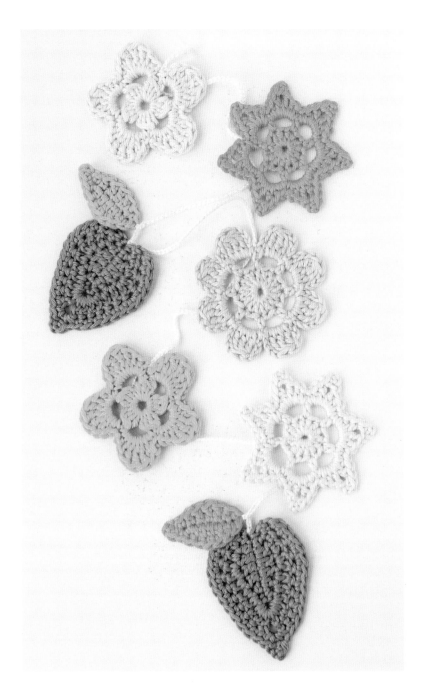

Tools and Materials

‣ Size 3.5mm (US E4) and 1.5mm (US 7) crochet hooks

‣ 50g balls (115m/126yd) of Rowan Cotton Glacé, one each in shades 865/Lipstick (yarn A), 730/Oyster (yarn B), 856/Mineral (yarn C), 845/Shell (yarn D), 844/Green Slate (yarn E) and 100g ball (400m/437yd) of DMC Petra size 5, one in shade 54460/Off-white (yarn F)

‣ Yarn needle

‣ Scissors

Yarn Substitution

This design will work well with any standard DK (worsted) weight cotton yarn or lighter, so that the motifs don't become too heavy for the garland. If using DK cotton yarn one 50g ball will be enough to complete a garland in a single colour.

Tension (Gauge)

6 rnds of circular motif worked in tr sts (12st inc each rnd) = 10cm (4in)

Finished Size

Flowers vary from 6–6.5cm (2⅜–2½in) diameter

Length of garland approx. 1.45m (57in)

PATTERN

All flower and leaf motifs are crocheted using the 3.5mm hook.

▷ 8-PETAL FLOWER MOTIF

Make 4, one each in yarns A, B, C and D.

Foundation ring and round 1: create an adjustable ring, ch3 (counts as first tr), 15tr into ring, close ring, ss into 3rd ch of starting ch3

Round 2: ch5 (counts as first htr, ch3), *miss 1st of prev rnd, [htr, ch3] into next st* rep from * to * 7 times, ss into 2nd ch of starting ch5

Round 3: ch1, *ss into next ch-sp, ch4, 3dtr-cl into same ch-sp, ch4, ss into same ch-sp* rep from * to * 8 times, ss into starting ch1, fasten off

▷ 5-PETAL FLOWER MOTIF

Make 4, one each in yarns A, B, C and D.

Foundation ring and round 1: create an adjustable ring, ch2, 3tr-cl (counts as first 4tr-cl), *ch4, 4tr-cl* rep from * to * 4 times, ch4, close ring, ss into top of 3tr-cl

Round 2: ch1, [dc, htr, tr, 3dtr, tr, htr, dc] into each ch-sp around, ss into first dc, fasten off

▷ 7-PETAL FLOWER MOTIF

Make 4, one each in yarns A, B, C and D.

Foundation ring and round 1: create an adjustable ring, ch2 (counts as first htr), 13htr into ring, close ring, ss into 2nd of starting ch2

Round 2: ch5, *miss 1st tr of prev rnd, [htr, ch3] into next st* rep from * to * 6 times, ss into 2nd of starting ch5

Round 3: ch1, [dc, htr, tr, ch3, dc into 3rd ch from hook, tr, htr, dc] into each ch-sp around, ss into first dc, fasten off

▷ LARGE LEAF MOTIF

Make 4 in yarn E.

Foundation chain: ch8

Round 1: starting in 2nd ch from hook *dc, htr, 3tr, htr, dc*, ch3 (leaf point), rotate the work and rep from * to * along the bottom of the foundation ch, **turn**

Round 2: ch1, dc, htr, tr, 2tr inc, 3tr, [3tr, ch2, 3tr] into leaf point ch-sp, 3tr, 2tr inc, tr, htr, dc, **turn**

Round 3: ch1, miss 1st tr of prev rnd, 2dc, 2dc inc into next 2 sts, 6dc, [dc, ch3, dc into 3rd ch from hook, dc] into leaf point ch-sp, 6dc, 2dc inc into next 2sts, 2dc, ss into next st, fasten off

▷ SMALL LEAF MOTIF

Make 4, one each in yarns A, B, C and D.

Foundation chain: ch8

Round 1: starting in 2nd ch from hook *dc, htr, 3tr, htr, dc*, [ch3, dc into 3rd ch from hook] leaf point, rotate the work and rep from * to * along the bottom of the foundation ch, fasten off

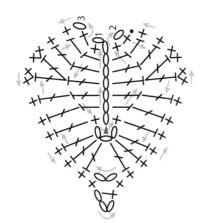

▷ BLOCKING

Using a press cloth, steam press each motif on reverse with a hot iron to these approx. sizes:

8-petal flower: 6.5cm (2½in) diameter

5-petal flower: 5.5cm (2¼in) diameter

7-petal flower: 6.5cm (2½in) diameter

Small leaf: 2 x 3.5cm (¾ x 1¼in)

Large leaf: 4.5 x 6cm (1¾ x 2⅜in)

▷ MAKING UP

Arrange the motifs according to the colour placement diagram and, beginning with the large leaf motif at the bottom, string the motifs together as follows:

First: using 1.5mm crochet hook, join yarn G in top of large leaf motif (opposite pointed tip), *†ch3, dc into top of small leaf motif, ch36, dc between 2 petals of 7-petal flower motif, ch40, dc between 2 petals of 5-petal flower motif, ch 40, dc between 2 petals of 8-petal flower motif†, ch40, dc into top of large leaf motif* rep from * to * 3 times, rep from † to † once more

Hanging loop: ch20, ss into same sp as last dc into 8-petal flower motif, fasten off securely and weave in loose ends

COLOUR PLACEMENT

▶ Lipstick
▶ Oyster
▶ Mineral
▶ Shell
▶ Green Slate

 TIPS AND TRICKS

This garland is designed to hang vertically but you could easily work a small hanging loop at either end to hang it in a swag if you prefer. To do so, join yarn F in first motif, ch20, ss into same sp as joined yarn, then continue stringing the garland motifs together as described. To make a multiple garland display as shown, you will also need a 50g ball of Rowan Cotton Glacé in shade 725/Ecru.

POLKA DOT STREAMER

These polka dot motifs were originally inspired by antique penny rugs that were hand sewn using woollen clothing scraps to create something new, beautiful and useful. I have chosen my favourite linen yarn to crochet these streamers, which comes in a stunning range of colours and I often have lots of leftovers that are perfect for crocheting polka dot motifs. Thanks to this streamer design, you can keep adding new polka dots whenever your stash of leftovers begins to overflow!

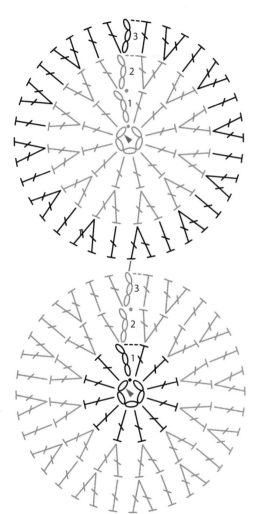

▽ Large-centre motif

△ Small-centre motif

Tools and Materials

- Size 3mm (US C2 or D3) crochet hook
- 50g balls (300m/330yds) of Yarn Stories Linen 3ply (laceweight), one each in shades 102/Off-white (yarn A), 406/Peach, 302/Emerald, 703/Yellow, 605/Sky, 310/Mint, 407/Magenta and 409/Orange
- Yarn needle
- Scissors

Yarn Substitution

This design will work well with almost any other weight of yarn, I would recommend 4ply or double knit (fingering or worsted) weight so that the streamer doesn't become too heavy.

Tension (Gauge)

Using 2 strands of yarn held together, 6 rnds in tr sts (12st increase each rnd) = 10cm (4in)

Finished Size

Polka dot motifs approx. 5cm (2in) diameter

Length of garland approx. 2.3m (2½yd)

COLOUR PLACEMENT

- Off-white
- Peach
- Emerald
- Yellow
- Sky
- Mint
- Magenta
- Orange

PATTERN

Each polka dot motif is worked with two strands of the same colour yarn held together throughout.

The main colour of the streamer is off-white (yarn A), which is used in round 1 of each small-centre motif and round 3 of each large-centre motif. The remaining colours (referred to as 'second colour' below) are then repeated in every seven motifs and six times throughout the streamer; refer to the colour placement diagram as a guide.

Begin the streamer with a small-centre motif then a large-centre motif, which is joined-as-you-go to the first motif. Then repeat a small-centre motif joining it to the second motif as you go. Continue in this way alternating between the two motif variations and repeating colours as described above.

▶ TIPS AND TRICKS

This is the perfect project for using up oddments of sock yarns or beautiful hand-dyed snippets that you can't bear to lose.

▷ SMALL-CENTRE MOTIF

Make 21 (first and every alternate motif).

Foundation ring: using yarn A and 3mm hook, ch5, ss to form ring

Round 1: ch3 (counts as first tr), 11tr into ring (12sts), fasten off invisibly

Round 2: join second colour in any st, ch3 (counts as first tr), tr into base of ch3, 2tr inc into each st around, ss to 3rd of starting ch3 (24sts)

First motif only round 3: ch3 (counts as first tr), tr into base of ch3, tr into next st *2tr inc, tr* rep from * to * around (36sts), fasten off invisibly

Third and every following alternate motif round 3: ch3 (counts as first tr), tr into base of ch3, tr into next st *2tr inc, tr* rep from * to * 6 times, jn into first st of rnd 3 of prev motif, rep from * to * 6 more times (36sts), fasten off invisibly

▷ LARGE-CENTRE MOTIF

Make 22 (second and every alternate motif).

Foundation ring: using second colour and 3mm hook, ch5, ss to form ring

Round 1: ch3 (counts as first tr), 11tr into ring, ss to 3rd of starting ch3 (12sts)

Round 2: ch3 (counts as first tr), tr into base of ch3, 2tr inc into each st around (24sts), fasten off invisibly

Round 3: join yarn A in any st, ch3 (counts as first tr), tr into base of ch3, tr into next st *2tr inc, tr* rep from * to * 6 times, jn into first st of rnd 3 of prev motif, rep from * to * 6 more times (36sts), fasten off invisibly

▷ BLOCKING

Using a press cloth, steam press on reverse with a hot iron.

PAPER FLOWER
CHARMS

These flower charms are made using a simple white paper twine, which creates a wonderful lacy effect even in the most basic crochet stitches. They are quick to crochet and can be used to decorate a bare branch all year round, or you could choose a more festive colour palette and give them as gifts during the holiday season.

Tools and Materials

- Size 3.5mm (US E4) crochet hook
- 120m (130yd) spool of Paperphine medium paper twine in white
- Three 2.5 x 6.5cm (1 x 2½in) fabric snippets per flower charm
- One 2.5cm (1in) button per flower charm
- Yarn needle
- Scissors

Yarn Substitution

This flower pattern is designed specifically for paper twine and does not translate well into other yarns.

Special Stitches

pf = place fabric snippet

Work as follows: take one fabric snippet and gather it at the centre, place the gather between your hook and working yarn, then tightly work a chain stitch to hold it in place.

Tension (Gauge)

The finished flower motif should measure 9cm (3½in) in diameter.

Finished Size

9 x 25cm (3½ x 10in)

TIPS AND TRICKS

Paper twine is a robust yarn and needs a firm hand to work it. It's not as delicate as you might think and is almost impossible to break or snap with just your hands. A tight grip is essential when working with paper twine to keep it under control, so that the tension in your finished flowers isn't too loose.

PATTERN

▷ FLOWER MOTIF

Foundation ring: using paper twine and 3.5mm hook, ch8, ss to form ring

Round 1: ch3 (counts as first tr), 29tr into ring, ss into 3rd of starting ch3

Round 2: ch4 (counts as first htr, ch2), *miss 1 st of prev rnd, htr into next st, ch2* rep from * to * 14 times, ss into 2nd of starting ch4

Round 3: *ss into next ch-sp, ch4, [dtr, tr, htr, dc] into ch-sp* rep from * to * 15 times, ss into starting ch of prev rnd, fasten off

▷ BLOCKING

Using a press cloth, gently steam press on the reverse with a hot iron, taking care not to allow the paper twine to become too hot or burn. If necessary, pull the petals into a neat shape whilst they are still warm (not hot), then press again and allow to cool.

▷ MAKING UP

Flower Stem

First: using a 3.5mm hook and paper twine, and leaving a 20cm (8in) tail of twine, *ch10, pf* rep from * to * twice, ch5, ss between any two petals of flower motif, fasten off.

Next: using the yarn needle and 20cm (8in) tail of yarn, sew a button to the end of the flower stem. Fasten off securely.

Add Hanging Loop

Join paper twine in the top of the 8th petal from the flower stem, ch5, pf, ch15, ss into 15th ch from hook. Fasten off and weave in loose ends.

GEOMETRY GARLAND

I think it's fair to say that I'm more than a little bit in love with crochet flowers, but as much as I adore pretty petals I can't resist some cute geometry and this garland is as cute as it gets! The Geometry Garland is a great way to teach little ones their shapes, making it the perfect nursery decoration. I've chosen a pretty Scandi-inspired, gender-neutral palette of colours so it would be the ideal baby shower gift for expectant parents who are keeping a secret.

Tools and Materials

- Size 3mm (US C2 or D3) and 1.5mm (US 7) crochet hooks
- 50g balls (155m/170yd) of DMC Natura Just Cotton, one each in shades N85/Giroflée (yarn A), N12/Light Green (yarn B), N05/Bleu Layette (yarn C), N53/Bleu Night (yarn D) and N81/Acanthe (yarn E)
- 100g ball (400m/437yd) of DMC Petra size 5, one in shade 54460/Off-white (yarn F)
- Yarn needle
- Scissors

Yarn Substitution

This design will work well with any standard 4ply (fingering) weight yarn or lighter, so that the motifs don't become too heavy for the garland.

Tension (Gauge)

7 rnds in tr sts (12st increase each rnd) = 10cm (4in)

Finished Size

Shapes vary from 4.5–6.5cm (1¾–2½in)

Length of garland approx. 1.6m (1¾yd)

TIPS AND TRICKS

You can crochet a colourful pennant garland using only the basic triangle motif. To make the triangles larger, simply continue working in the set pattern beyond row 7 until the pennant is the required size. Alternatively, to create a stars and moon garland, combine the star motif with a simple circle motif.

PATTERN

▷ HEXAGON MOTIF

Make 3.

Foundation ring: using yarn B and 3mm hook, ch5, ss to form ring

Round 1: ch3 (counts as first tr), 11tr into ring, ss into 3rd of starting ch3

Round 2: ch3 (counts as first tr), tr into base of ch3, *†[tr, ch2, tr] into next st†, 2tr inc into next st* rep from * to * 5 times, rep from † to † once more, ss into 3rd of starting ch3

Round 3: ch3 (counts as first tr), tr into 2sts, *†[tr, ch2, dc into 2nd ch from hook, tr] into corner ch-sp†, tr into 4sts* rep from * to * 5 times, rep from † to † once more, tr into next st, fasten off invisibly

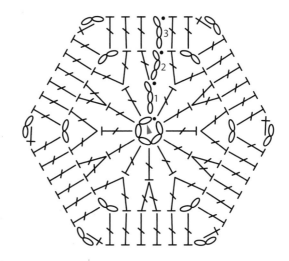

▷ TRIANGLE MOTIF

Make 3.

Foundation ring: using yarn E and 3mm hook, create an adjustable ring

Row 1: ch3 (counts as first tr), 2tr into ring, close adjustable ring, **turn**

Row 2: ch3 (counts as first tr), tr into 2sts, 2tr inc into 3rd of starting ch3 of prev row, **turn**

Row 3: ch3 (counts as first tr), tr into 4sts, 2tr inc into 3rd of starting ch3 of prev row, **turn**

Rows 4–7: rows 2 and 3 set the pattern for the triangle motif, continue increasing in this way in rows 4 to 7, fasten off

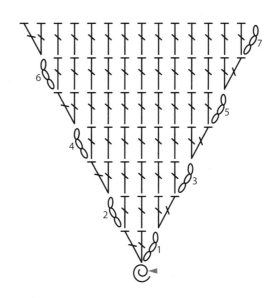

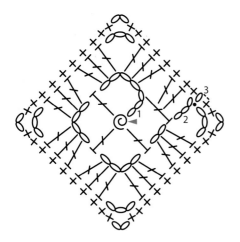

▷ DIAMOND MOTIF

Make 3.

Foundation ring: using yarn C and 3mm hook, create an adjustable ring

Round 1: ch7 (counts as first tr, ch4), [tr, ch4] twice into ring, [tr, ch2] once into ring, close adjustable ring, tr into 3rd of starting ch7

Round 2: ch3 (counts as first tr), 2tr into next sp, *[3tr, ch3, 3tr] into corner ch-sp* rep from * to * 3 times, [3tr, ch3] into last ch-sp, ss into 3rd of starting ch3

Round 3: ch1, dc into base of ch1, dc into 5sts, *†[2dc, ch2, 2dc] into corner ch-sp†, dc into 6sts* rep from * to * 3 times, rep from † to † once more, fasten off invisibly

▷ STAR MOTIF

Make 3.

Foundation ring: using yarn D and 3mm hook, ch5, ss to form ring

Round 1: ch6 (counts as first tr, ch3), [tr, ch3] 4 times into ring, ss into 3rd of starting ch6

Round 2: ch1, [dc, tr, dtr, ch3, dc into first ch of ch3, dtr, tr, dc] into each ch-sp around, ss into first dc, fasten off

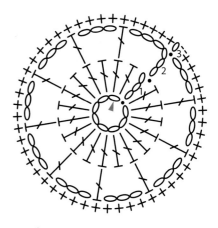

▷ WHEEL MOTIF

Make 4.

Foundation ring: using yarn A and 3mm hook, ch8, ss to form ring,

Round 1: ch3 (counts as first tr), 19tr into ring, ss into 3rd of starting ch3

Round 2: ch6 (counts as first tr, ch3), *miss 1st of prev rnd, [tr, ch3] into next st* rep from * to * 9 times, ss into 3rd of starting ch6

Round 3: ch1, dc into base of ch1, *4dc into ch-sp, dc into tr st of prev rnd* rep from * to * 9 times, 4dc into next ch-sp, fasten off invisibly

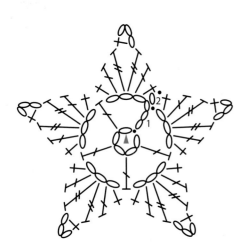

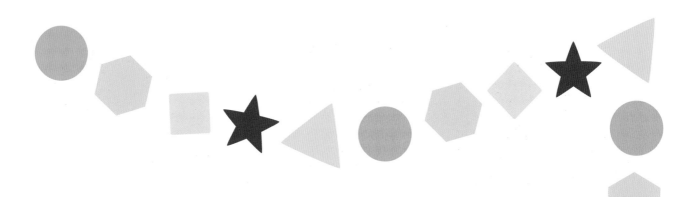

▷ BLOCKING

Using a press cloth, steam press each motif on reverse with a hot iron to the correct size:

Wheel motif: 5.5cm (2¼in) diameter

Hexagon motif: 5cm (2in) edge to edge

Diamond motif: 4.5cm (1¾in) edge to edge

Star motif: 6cm (2⅜in) point to point

Triangle motif: 6.5cm (2½in) point to point

▷ MAKING UP

Using yarn F and 1.5mm hook, work by stringing motifs together from right to left as follows:

First hanging loop: ch10, ss to form ring, ch1, 20dc into ring, ss into first dc

Place first wheel motif: ch20, dc into top of any edge st of wheel motif

†Place triangle motif: ch30, dc into top rightmost st (ch st) of triangle motif, *ch3, miss one st, dc into next st of triangle motif* rep from * to * 7 times

Place star motif: ch30, dc into any point of star motif

Place diamond motif: ch40, dc into any corner st of diamond motif

Place hexagon motif: ch35, dc into 2nd ch st of any corner of hexagon motif, then work [ch3, miss one st, dc into next tr st, ch3] 3 times, ch3, dc into 2nd ch st of second corner of hexagon motif

Place next wheel motif: ch35, dc into any edge st of wheel motif†

Place remaning motifs: rep from † to † until all motifs are strung into the garland

Second hanging loop: ch30, ss into 10th ch from hook to form a ring, 20dc into ring, fasten off invisibly and weave in loose ends

COLOUR PLACEMENT

▶ Giroflée
▶ Light Green
▶ Bleu Layette
▶ Bleu Night
▶ Acanthe

BLOSSOM WREATH

This sweet, vintage-inspired floral wreath is an ideal project to indulge your love of crochet flowers. The wreath is wrapped in a luxury alpaca yarn and the flowers are crocheted using linen, which helps to ensure they keep their three-dimensional shape. I have chosen a fresh spring palette of mint, orange, pink, yellow, ivory and duck egg blue that is a little bit retro, making this wreath perfectly granny chic!

Tools and Materials

- Size 3mm (US C2 or D3) crochet hook
- 50g (300m/330yd) balls of Yarn Stories Linen 3ply (laceweight), one each in shades 508/Pink (yarn A), 703/Yellow (yarn B), 102/Off-white (yarn C), 409/Orange (yarn D) and 310/Mint (yarn E)
- 50g (40m/43yd) ball of Wool and the Gang Wooly Bully Alpaca, one in shade Mr Blue Sky (yarn F)
- 17cm (6½in) diameter wreath form
- Pale pink velvet ribbon, 30cm (12in) long
- One 2cm (¾in) button
- Yarn needle
- Scissors
- Sewing needle and thread to coordinate with ribbon
- Adhesive tape or glue

Yarn Substitution

Any beautifully textured yarn will be ideal for wrapping the wreath form, and any 4ply (fingering) yarn or lighter will work well for the flowers, to ensure that they do not become too large for the wreath size.

Special Stitches

pc = popcorn stitch

In this pattern popcorn stitches are worked using 5 treble stitches and chain stitches worked afterwards are not counted as part of the popcorn stitch.

Tension (Gauge)

Using 2 strands of Yarn Stories Linen yarn held together, 6 rnds in tr sts (12st increase each rnd) = 10cm (4in)

Finished Size

17cm (6½in) diameter (excluding hanging loop)

PATTERN

Each flower and leaf motif is worked using the 3mm hook, with two strands of the same colour of Yarn Stories Linen yarn held together throughout.

▷ MEDIUM FLOWER MOTIF

Make 3, one each in yarns A and D, C and B, and A and C.

Foundation ring: ch6, ss to form ring

Round 1: ch2, [pc, ch3] 5 times into ring, ss into top of first pc, fasten off

Round 2: join yarn in any ch-sp, ch1, then work [dc, htr, tr, 3dtr, tr, htr, dc] into each ch-sp around, ss into first dc, fasten off

▷ SMALL FLOWER MOTIF

Make 5, two in yarn D and one each in yarns A, B and C.

Foundation ring: ch4, ss to form ring

Round 1: [ch5, ss into ring] 5 times

Round 2: 8dc into each ch-sp around, ss into first dc, fasten off

▷ LEAF MOTIF

Make 8 in yarn E.

Foundation chain: ch8

Round 1: starting in 2nd ch from hook *dc, htr, 3tr, htr, dc*, [ch3, dc into 3rd ch from hook] leaf point, rotate the work and rep from * to * along the bottom of the foundation ch, fasten off

▷ LARGE FLOWER MOTIF

Make 3, one each in yarns A and B, B and C, and D and A.

Foundation ring: ch6, ss to form ring

Round 1: ch2 (counts as first htr), 7htr into ring, ss into 2nd of starting ch2

Round 2: ch6 (counts as first htr, ch4), *htr, ch4* rep from * to * 7 times, ss into 2nd of starting ch6, fasten off

Round 3: join yarn in any ch-sp, ch1, then work [ss into ch-sp, ch4, 5dtr, 2tr, htr, dc] into each ch-sp around, ss into base of first ch4, fasten off

▷ MAKING UP

To ensure the flower and leaf motifs retain their three-dimensional shape, **do not** block or press.

Wrap Wreath Form

Using yarn F, tape the end of the yarn on the back of the wreath form, or glue in place. Begin wrapping the yarn around the wreath form ensuring that each yarn wrap is neatly and tightly gathered next to the one before it on the inside of the wreath (the wreath form will still be visible on the outer edge after the first layer of wrapping). Wrap a second layer of yarn around the wreath form and begin to fill in the gaps on the outer edge. Then continue wrapping for a third layer to fill in any remaining gaps. Fasten off securely at the back.

Add Hanging Loop

Fold the velvet ribbon over by 1cm (⅜in) at one end, then wrap this end tightly around the top of the wreath. Using the sewing needle and coordinating thread, secure the folded end to the main length of ribbon with a few small stitches, then add a few small stitches to anchor it to the wreath.

At the opposite end of the ribbon, fold over 1cm (⅜in), then fold over another 4cm (1⅝in) to create a loop; secure with a few small stitches. Sew the button in place over your stitches and fasten off.

Add Flowers

Using one strand of coordinating linen yarn, sew each flower and leaf motif into place, using the photograph of the finished wreath as a guide to placement. Fasten off and weave in loose ends.

DAY DREAMER
DREAMCATCHER

Dreamcatchers originate from the Ojibwe people of North America who believed they would protect sleeping children from bad dreams. Originally they were hung from the hoop of a cradleboard where the bad dreams would become entangled in the delicate web-like net, allowing only good thoughts to pass through to the dreamer. This belief has now been adopted and adapted by many people across the world and I keep one hanging in my studio to remind me not to dwell on negative or uncreative thoughts.

△ **Dreamcatcher web**

Tools and Materials

- Size 3mm (US C2 or D3) crochet hook
- 50g ball (274m/300yd) of Yarn Stories Linen 3ply (laceweight), one in 102/Off-white
- 17.5cm (7in) metal ring (such as a lampshade ring)
- Six 2.5cm (1in) wide fabric ribbons measuring approx. 110cm (43in) long (can be made from one long quarter of quilting cotton fabric)
- 15 mother-of-pearl buttons 12mm (½in) diameter
- Double-sided tape and craft scissors
- Yarn needle
- Scissors
- Blocking pins
- Sprung pegs (large enough to grip the metal ring)
- Sewing needle and thread to coordinate with fabric

Yarn Substitution

Any standard 4ply (fingering) weight yarn can easily be substituted for the stated yarn; however, checking your tension carefully beforehand is strongly recommended.

Tension (Gauge)

Using 2 strands of yarn held together, 6 rnds in tr sts (12st increase each rnd) = 10cm (4in)

Finished Size

18 x 86cm (7 x 34in)

PATTERN

▷ DREAMCATCHER WEB

Foundation ring: using 3mm hook and two strands of yarn held together ch8, ss to form ring

Round 1: ch3, 2dtr-cl (counts as first 3dtr-cl), *ch3, 3dtr-cl* rep from * to * 7 times, ch3, ss into top of first 2dtr-cl

Round 2: ch1, [dc, htr, tr, ch2, tr, htr, dc] into each ch-sp around, ss into first dc, fasten off yarn

Round 3: join yarn in any ch-sp of prev rnd, ch5 (counts as first dtr, ch1), [dtr, ch1] 4 times into same ch-sp, [dtr, ch1] 5 times into each ch-sp around, ss into 4th of starting ch5

Round 4: ch3 (counts as first tr), *†2tr inc into next 3sts, tr into next st, ch2†, tr into next st* rep from * to * 7 times, rep from † to † once more, ss into 3rd of starting ch3

Round 5: ch1, dc into base of ch1, *†htr, tr, [tr, dtr, ch1] into next st, [dtr, tr] into next st, tr, htr, dc, ss into ch-sp†, dc* rep from * to * 7 times, rep from † to † once more, ss into first dc, fasten off

Round 6: join yarn in any ch-sp of prev rnd, ch6 (counts as first dtr, ch2), [(tr, ch2) twice, dtr] into same ch-sp, *†ch3, dtr2tog over next 2 dc sts of prev rnd, ch3†, [dtr, ch2, (tr, ch2) twice, dtr] into next ch-sp* rep from * to * 7 times, rep from † to † once more, ss into 4th of starting ch6

Round 7: ch6 (counts as first tr, ch3), *†[tr, ch2] into next st†, [tr, ch3] into next 4 sts* rep from * to * 7 times, rep from † to † once more, [tr, ch3] into next 3 sts, ss into 3rd of starting ch6

Round 8: ch1, dc into base of ch1, ch3, [dc, ch3] into each tr st of prev rnd, ss into first dc, fasten off and weave in loose ends

▷ BLOCKING

Steam block the dreamcatcher web to 16.5cm (6½in) diameter.

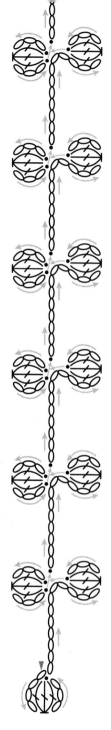

△ **Crochet streamers**

▷ CROCHET STREAMERS

Make 4 streamers 2 long and 2 short.

Repeats for the streamer buds are shown as: long (short).

First: using 3mm hook and two strands of yarn held together, leave a 20cm (8in) tail of yarn, ch4, 3tr-cl into 4th ch from hook, ch3, ss into base of cl st

Next: *ch12, 3tr-cl into 4th ch from hook, ch3, ss into base of cl st, ss into next ch, ch3, 3tr-cl into base of cl st, ch3, ss into base of cl st, **turn work** and ss between 2 buds just created* rep from * to * 15 (10) times, ch12, fasten off leaving a 20cm (8in) tail of yarn

Add Buttons

Using a yarn needle and the 20cm (8in) tail of yarn at the beginning of the crochet streamer, sew a button to the first bud of each streamer. Sew another three buttons onto random buds of the long streamers and two onto random buds of the short streamers.

▷ MAKING UP

Fabric-wrap Metal Ring

Wrap a 7.5cm (3in) section of the metal ring with double-sided tape. At the halfway point of the taped section, secure one end of a fabric strip at a 45-degree angle and start to wrap it around the metal ring, half overlapping itself with each wrap to cover the ring completely (one fabric strip should be sufficient to do this). When you reach your start point, secure the end of the fabric strip with a small piece of double-sided tape, then bind in place with a length of yarn.

Add Dreamcatcher Web

Use the sprung pegs to hold the dreamcatcher web in place inside the metal ring. Using the yarn needle threaded with a 1.5m (60in) length of doubled yarn, thread it through the top of any double crochet stitch of the last round of the dreamcatcher web and tie it securely onto the metal ring. Working whip stitch around the metal ring and through the top of

 TIPS AND TRICKS

It is easy to make your own fabric ribbons from a long quarter of standard quilting cotton fabric measuring approx. 25 x 112cm (10 x 44in). Here, I've used Meadow Blossoms organic cotton in white from the Lotus Pond collection by Rae Hoekstra. Along the fabric selvedge, mark 2.5cm (1in) intervals with a fabric pen, then take your scissors and cut approx. the same distance into the fabric at these points. Tear the fabric into strips and discard any loose threads. Steam press your fabric ribbons with a hot iron before use.

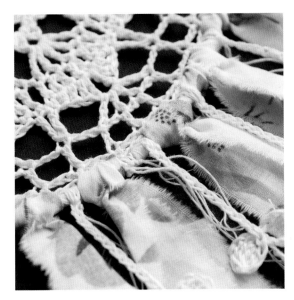
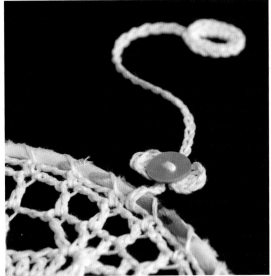

each double crochet stitch, sew the web to the ring, ensuring even stitch spacing all the way around. Fasten off securely.

Add Fabric Ribbons

Take a fabric ribbon and fold it in half so that there is a loop at the centre. Pass the loop around the dreamcatcher ring and through a 3ch crochet space at the bottom edge of the dreamcatcher web (your crochet hook will be useful in tight spaces here). Pass the ends of the fabric ribbon through the loop and pull the loop tightly closed.

Repeat for the remaining four fabric ribbons, adding them to alternate 3ch crochet spaces at the bottom edge of the dreamcatcher web.

Trim the fabric ribbons to varying lengths to create a deep V shape at the bottom.

Add Crochet Streamers

Using a yarn needle and the 20cm (8in) tail of yarn at the end of the long crochet streamers, securely sew each one either side of the central fabric ribbon. Repeat with the short crochet streamers placing them between the outer fabric ribbons. Fasten off.

Add Hanging Loop

First: using 3mm hook and two strands of yarn held together, leave a 30cm (12in) tail of yarn, ch6

Next: pass crochet chain through the top of the dreamcatcher web and around the metal ring, ss into first ch to secure in place

Next: ch6, 3tr-cl into 4th ch from hook, ch3, ss into base of cl st, ss into next ch, ch3, 3tr-cl into base of cl st, ch3, ss into base of cl st, **turn work** and ss between 2 buds just created

Next: ch30 (or to desired length), ss into 8th ch from hook to form ring

Next: 14dc into ring, ss into first dc, fasten off and weave in loose ends

To finish: using a yarn needle and the 30cm (12in) tail of yarn, sew the last button between the 2 buds at the beginning of the hanging loop

OVERSIZED
WALLFLOWER
HANGING

These oversized wallflowers are a fabulous way to add a touch of tactile crochet to your living space. While they can be used individually as trivets around your kitchen and dining table, they look absolutely stunning when joined together to create a colour-blocked geometric wall hanging.

Tools and Materials

▸ Size 12mm (US P17) crochet hook

▸ 500g cones (99.5m/108yd) of
Wool And The Gang, Jersey
Be Good, one each in shades
True Blue, Spearmint Green and
Hot Latte

▸ Yarn needle, wide-eyed blunt

▸ Scissors

▸ Sewing needle and strong thread

Yarn Substitution

If you substitute the yarn with
another jersey yarn, be sure to
use the correct hook, as jersey
yarns can vary greatly between
manufacturers. This pattern
will scale well to suit any hook
and yarn size you choose, but
remember that using a different
size hook and yarn will alter the
finished size of your flowers.

Tension

Individual wallflowers should
measure 24.5cm (9¾in) in diameter
when blocked.

Finished Size

The wallflower hanging should
measure 67cm (26½in) long by 1m
(39½in) wide.

PATTERN

▷ WALLFLOWERS

Make 9, three each in Spearmint Green, True Blue and Hot Latte.

Foundation ring: using jersey yarn and 12mm hook, ch8, ss to form ring

Round 1: ch3 (counts as first tr), 19tr into ring, ss into 3rd of starting ch3

Round 2: ch2, tr into next st (counts as first tr2tog), *ch3, tr2tog over next 2sts* rep from * to * 9 times, ch3, ss into top of first tr2tog

Round 3: ch1, [dc, htr, tr, ch1, tr, htr, dc] into each ch-sp around, ss into first dc, fasten off yarn and weave in loose ends

▷ BLOCKING

First insert your fingers or thumbs into the ch-sp of opposing petals and pull the flower to stretch out the motif; do this with all petals. Then, lay the flower face down and gently steam press on reverse, allowing the steam to penetrate through to the front of the flower. Gently pull the flower into a neat shape, even out the petals and allow to dry fully.

▷ MAKING UP

Joining Flowers

Lay the flowers face down in the colour arrangement shown in the finished photograph. Then, with the sewing needle and strong thread, use a whip stitch to join the petals together at the points marked with a red star on the chart, ensuring that the stitches will not be seen from the right side.

Displaying Hanging

Small panel pins are ideal for displaying the wallflower hanging as they will be hidden amongst the flowers once the display is complete. Five panel pins will be enough for this hanging, one for each flower motif along the top edge. Once you have marked the positions of the panel pins on the wall, hammer each into place leaving 1cm (⅜in) protruding, which is just enough to hold the hanging without them being seen.

 TIPS AND TRICKS

When sewing in loose ends of jersey yarn, to easily thread it onto the wide-eyed needle first unroll it. Once flat, fold it in half and thread it through the eye; a few centimetres will be enough it hold it securely.

SIMPLE FOLK CIRCLE POTHOLDER

If you have never crocheted a potholder before, this simple granny circle is a great place to start. Just as easy to work as your basic granny square, it can be quickly crocheted in a couple of hours. It is made using a beautifully soft yet sturdy mercerized cotton, which is an ideal fibre for daily use in the kitchen as it can withstand regular washing and is resilient to high temperatures. Practical and pretty! What more do you need from a potholder?

Tools and Materials

▸ Size 3mm (US C2 or D3) crochet hook

▸ 100g balls (280m/306yd) of DMC Petra size 3, one each in shades Ecru (yarn A), 5742/ Yellow (yarn B), 53814/Emerald (yarn C), 54463/Sky (yarn D), 5722/Orange (yarn E) and 54461/ Pale Pink (yarn F)

▸ Yarn needle

▸ Scissors

Yarn Substitution

Any standard 4ply (fingering) weight cotton yarn can easily be substituted for the stated yarn; however, checking your tension carefully beforehand is strongly recommended.

Tension (Gauge)

7 rnds in tr sts (12st increase each rnd) = 10cm (4in)

Finished Size

18cm (7in) diameter

PATTERN

▷ FRONT AND BACK PANELS

The back and front panels of the simple folk circle potholder are worked in the same stitch and colour arrangement but, for the front section, leave a 30cm (12in) tail of yarn before beginning.

Foundation ring: using yarn A and 3mm hook, ch5, ss to form ring

Round 1: ch4 (counts as first tr, ch1), [tr, ch1] 7 times into ring, ss into 3rd of starting ch4

Round 2: ss into next ch-sp, ch3 (counts as first tr), [tr, ch1] into same sp, [2tr shell, ch1] into each ch-sp around, ss into 3rd of starting ch3

Round 3: ch4 (counts as first tr, ch1), [3tr shell, ch1] into 7 ch-sps, 2tr into last ch-sp, ss into 3rd of starting ch4, fasten off

◁ **Front and back panels with edging**

Round 4: join yarn B in any ch-sp, ch3 (counts as first tr), [tr, ch1, 2tr shell, ch1] into same ch-sp, [2tr shell, ch1] twice into each ch-sp around, ss into 3rd of starting ch3, fasten off

Round 5: join yarn A in any ch-sp, ch3 (counts as first tr), [2tr shell, ch1] into same sp, [3tr shell, ch1] into each ch-sp around, ss into 3rd of starting ch3, fasten off

Round 6: join yarn C in any ch-sp and work as given for rnd 4, fasten off

Round 7: join yarn D in any ch-sp, ch3 (counts as first tr), tr into same sp, 2tr shell into each ch-sp around, ss into 3rd of starting ch3, fasten off

Round 8: join yarn E between any 2tr shells of prev rnd, ch3 (counts as first tr), [tr, ch1] into same sp, [2tr shell, ch1] between 2tr shells around, ss into 3rd of starting ch3, fasten off

Round 9: join yarn A in any ch-sp, ch3 (counts as first tr), 2tr shell into same sp, 3tr shell into each ch-sp around, ss into 3rd of starting ch3

Round 10: ch3 (counts as first tr), 3tr shell into each sp between 3tr shells of prev rnd, 2tr into last sp, ss into 3rd of starting ch3, fasten off

Round 11: join yarn D between any 3tr shells of prev rnd and work as given for rnd 5, fasten off

Round 12: join yarn F in any ch-sp of prev rnd and work as given for rnd 5, fasten off

Round 13: join yarn B in any ch-sp and work as given for rnd 4, fasten off

▷ MAKING UP

Join Front and Back Panels

Weave in loose ends of front and back panels. Lay front and back panels together, with WS facing, and line up the stitch pattern at the centre. Using the yarn needle and 30cm (12in) tail of yarn, sew the two panels together using a whip stitch through the centre hole and tr sts of rnd 1; fasten off yarn between the two panels and weave in the loose end.

Edging

All of the edging sts are worked through corresponding ch-sps of both panels together.

First: with front panel facing, line up the stitch pattern at the edge of the panels

Round 1: join yarn A in ch-sp in the centre of any 2tr shell rep of prev rnd, ch1, dc into same sp, *6tr shell into next ch-sp, dc into next ch-sp* rep from * to * 5 times

Hanging loop: 3dc into next ch-sp, dc into next ch-sp, ch15, working backwards ss into the first dc after the prev 6tr shell, ss into the last tr st of prev shell, working forwards 20dc into ch-sp, ss into same space as last dc before 15ch

Continue round 1: rep from * to * 26 times, 6tr into next ch-sp, ss into first dc, fasten off and weave in loose ends

▷ BLOCKING

Using a press cloth, steam block on reverse with a hot iron.

FABULOUS ROSE POTHOLDER

This potholder design was inspired by all those gorgeous little rose motifs in Irish crochet with their layers upon layers of densely worked petals. It is a motif that I find endlessly inspiring, and here I am paying homage to Irish crochet by working the rose panel in traditional white, then adding a pop of colour with a sunny yellow background. This is a must have for any potholder wall.

▽ **Front panel: centre**

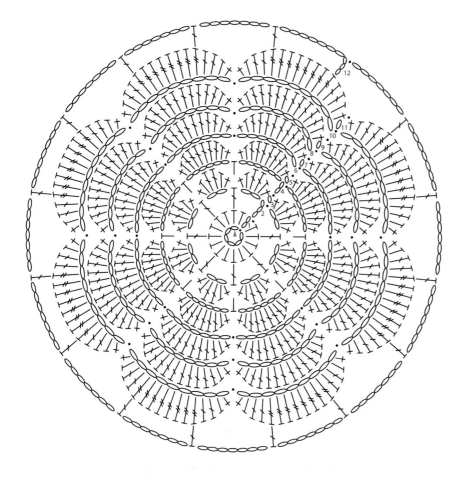

Tools and Materials

‣ Size 3mm (US C2 or D3) crochet hook

‣ 100g balls (280m/306yd) of DMC Petra, size 3, one each in shades B5200/White (yarn A), 5742/Yellow (yarn B) and Ecru (yarn C)

‣ Yarn needle

‣ Scissors

Yarn Substitution

Any standard 4ply (fingering) weight cotton yarn can easily be substituted for the stated yarn; however, checking your tension carefully beforehand is strongly recommended.

Tension (Gauge)

7 rnds in tr sts (12st increase each rnd) = 10cm (4in)

Finished Size

19.5cm (7¾in) diameter (excluding hanging loop)

TIPS AND TRICKS

For a more colourful alternative to the beautiful white rose, crochet each round of petals in a different colour and layer onto a white back panel to show them off to their best. Or choose several shades in your favourite colour for a fabulous ombré effect.

PATTERN

▷ FRONT PANEL

Foundation ring: using yarn A and 3mm hook, leave a 30cm (12in) tail of yarn, ch6, ss to form ring

Round 1: ch2 (counts as first htr), 15htr into ring, ss to 2nd of starting ch2

Round 2: ch5 (counts as first tr, ch2), *miss 1 st of prev rnd, tr into next st, ch2* rep from * to * 7 times, ss into 3rd of starting ch5

Round 3: ch1, [dc, htr, 2tr, htr, dc] into each ch-sp around, ss into first dc

Round 4: ch8 (counts as first htr, ch6), *htr between dc sts of next 2 petals of prev rnd, ch6* rep from * to * 7 times, ss into 3rd of starting ch8

Round 5: ch1, [dc, htr, 6tr, htr, dc] into each ch-sp around, ss into first dc

Round 6: *ch7, ss between dc sts of next 2 petals* rep from * to * 8 times

Round 7: ch1, [dc, htr, 8tr, htr, dc] into each ch-sp around, ss into first dc

Round 8: *ch8, ss between (dc sts of) next 2 petals* rep from * to * 8 times

Round 9: ch1, [dc, htr, 10tr, htr, dc] into each ch-sp around, ss into first dc

Round 10: *ch9, ss between dc sts of next 2 petals* rep from * to * 8 times

Round 11: ch1, [dc, htr, 2tr, 8dtr, 2tr, htr, dc] into each ch-sp around, ss into first dc, fasten off

Round 12: join yarn A in 5th st of any petal of prev rnd, ch10 (counts as first tr, ch7), then work [tr, ch7] into 12th st of same petal, then [tr, ch7] into 5th and 12th sts of every petal around, ss into 3rd of starting ch10

Round 13: ch1, [dc, htr, 8tr, htr, dc] into each ch-sp around, ss into first dc, fasten off

Round 14: join yarn A in 4th st of any petal of prev rnd, ch7 (counts as first tr, ch4), [tr, ch4] into 9th st of same petal, *[tr, ch4] into 4th and 9th sts of next petal* rep from * to * 15 times, ss into 3rd of starting ch7

Round 15: ch1, [dc, htr, 3tr, htr, dc] into each ch-sp around, ss into first dc

Round 16: *ch5, ss between (dc sts of) next 2 petals* rep from * to * 32 times

Round 17: rep rnd 15

Round 18: rep rnd 16, fasten off

▽ **Front panel: outer**

Note: Rnd 12 repeated from previous chart

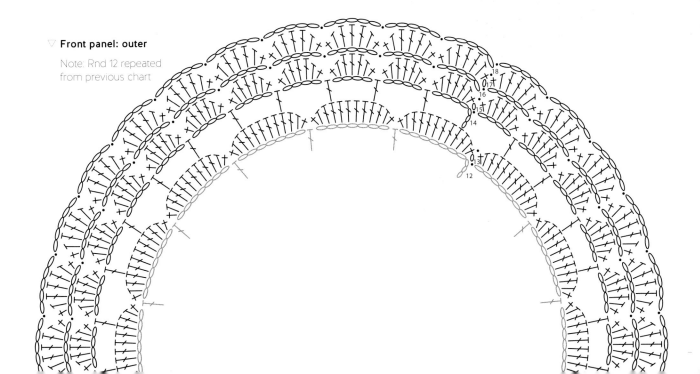

▷ BACK PANEL

Foundation ring: using yarn B and 3mm hook ch6, ss to form ring

Round 1: ch3 (counts as first tr), 11tr into ring, ss into 3rd of starting ch3 (12sts)

Round 2: ch3 (counts as first tr), tr into base of ch3, 2tr inc into each st around, ss into 3rd of starting ch3 (24sts)

Round 3: ch3 (counts as first tr), tr into base of ch3, tr into next st, *2tr inc, tr* rep from * to * around, ss into 3rd of starting ch3 (36sts)

Round 4: ch3 (counts as first tr), tr into base of ch3, tr into next 2 sts, *2tr inc, tr into 2 sts* rep from * to * around, ss into 3rd of starting ch3 (48sts)

Round 5: ch3 (counts as first tr), tr into base of ch3, tr into next 3 sts, *2tr inc, tr into 3 sts* rep from * to * around, ss into 3rd of starting ch3 (60sts)

Round 6–12: rnds 1 to 5 set the pattern for the back panel, continue increasing in this way for rnds 6 to 12 (144sts) to create a flat circle, fasten off invisibly

▽ **Back panel**

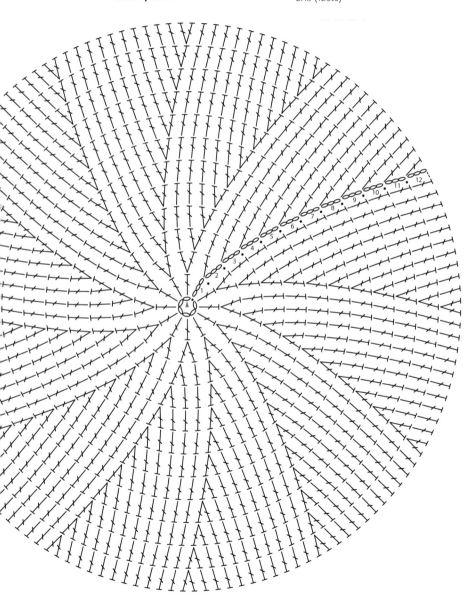

▷ MAKING UP

Join Front and Back Panels

Weave in loose ends of front and back panels. Lay front and back panels together with WS facing, and line up the stitch pattern at the centre. Using the yarn needle and 30cm (12in) tail of yarn, sew the two panels together using a whip stitch through the centre hole and sts of rnd 1; fasten off yarn between the two panels and weave in the loose end.

Edging

All edging sts are worked through corresponding sts and ch-sps of both front and back panels together.

Round 1: with RS of front panel facing, join yarn C in any ch-sp of front panel and top of tr st of back section, ch1, dc into same sp, dc into 2sts and same ch-sp, 2dc inc into next st and same ch-sp, *†dc into 5sts and next ch-sp†, dc into 3sts and next ch-sp, 2dc inc into next st and same ch-sp* rep from * to * 15 times, rep from † to † once more, ss into first dc (160sts)

Round 2: ch1, dc into base of ch1, dc into 8sts, 2dc inc, dc into 3sts, ch15, miss 4sts of prev rnd, dc into 2sts, *2dc inc, dc into 9sts* rep from * to * 14 times, 2dc inc, ss into first dc (176sts)

Round 3: ch1, dc into base of ch1, dc into 13sts, 20dc into ch-sp, dc into next and each st around, fasten off invisibly and weave in loose ends

▷ BLOCKING

To avoid crushing the flower petals, steam block only; **do not** press.

▽ **Edging**

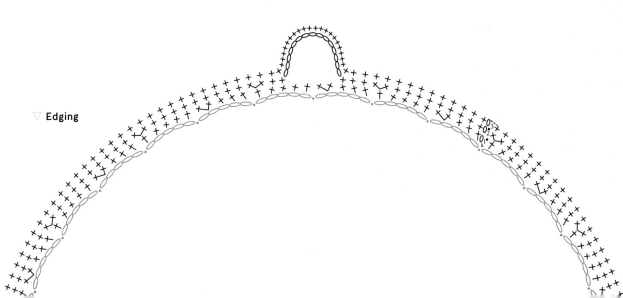

FILET DAISY POTHOLDER

Traditional filet crochet designs are most often seen worked in rows using treble crochet and chain stitches to create a mesh-like grid, and by filling the spaces with more treble stitches an array of interesting patterns can be produced. However, the same idea can just as easily be applied to circular motifs, using densely placed treble stitches and increases separated by that familiar open mesh work as can be seen on my Filet Daisy Potholder. It is worked in two layers and the petals of the daisy motif are aligned with joining double crochet stitches to maximize the beautiful filet effect.

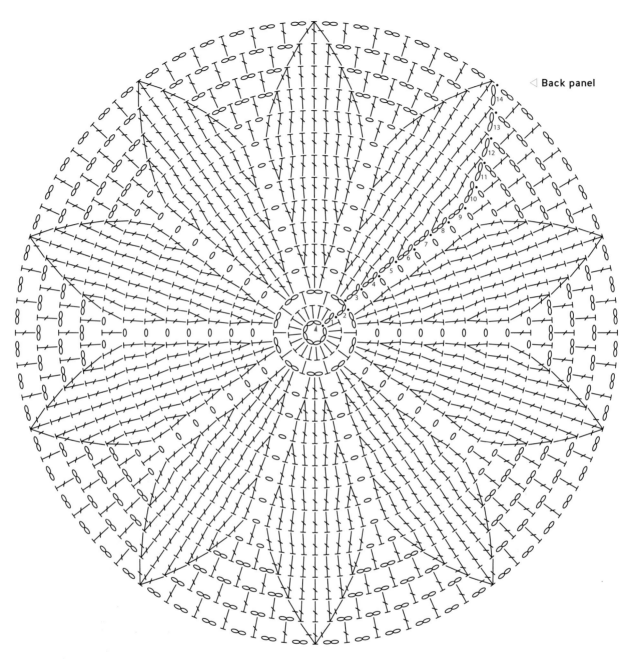

◁ **Back panel**

 TIPS AND TRICKS

When you come to join the two panels together with jdc stitches, take care to ensure that you are working into the correct row of the back panel. If you are unsure, you could mark the appropriate stitches on each row with a different coloured stitch marker or scrap yarn. Use the symbols shown on the front panel chart as a guide.

Tools and Materials

‣ Size 3mm (US C2 or D3) crochet hook
‣ 100g balls (280m/306yd) of DMC Petra, size 3, one each in shades Ecru (yarn A), 5722/ Orange (yarn B) and 54461/ Pale Pink (yarn C)
‣ Yarn needle
‣ Scissors

Yarn Substitution

Any standard 4ply (fingering) weight cotton yarn can easily be substituted for the stated yarn; however, checking your tension carefully beforehand is strongly recommended.

Special Stitches

jdc = a double crochet stitch to join the front and back sections of the potholder worked as follows: double crochet into corresponding ch-sp on same round of back section, either immediately before or after tr2tog st of the petal motif

Tension (Gauge)

7 rnds in tr sts (12st increase each rnd) = 10cm (4in)

Finished Size

23cm (9in) diameter (excluding hanging loop)

PATTERN

▷ BACK PANEL

Foundation ring: using yarn A and 3mm hook ch8, ss to form ring

Round 1: ch2 (counts as first htr), 19htr into ring, ss into 2nd of starting ch2

Round 2: ch4 (counts as first htr, ch2), *miss one st of prev rnd, htr into next st, ch2* rep from * to * 9 times, ss into 2nd of starting ch4

Round 3: ss into ch-sp, ch3 (counts as first tr), 2tr into ch-sp, *ch1, 3tr into next ch-sp * rep from * to * 9 times, ch1, ss into 3rd of starting ch3

Round 4: ch3, tr into base of ch3 (counts as first 2tr inc), tr, 2tr inc, *ch1, miss ch-sp of prev rnd, 2tr inc, tr, 2tr inc * rep from * to * 9 times, ch1, ss into 3rd of starting ch3

Round 5: ch3 (counts as first tr), tr into 4sts, *ch1, miss ch-sp of prev rnd, tr into 5sts* rep from * to * 9 times, ch1, ss into 3rd of starting ch3

Round 6: ch3, tr into base of ch3 (counts as first 2tr inc), tr into 3sts, 2tr inc, *ch1, miss ch-sp of prev rnd, 2tr inc, 3tr, 2tr inc* rep from * to * 9 times, ch1, ss into 3rd of starting ch3

Round 7: ch3 (counts as first tr), tr into 6sts, *ch1, miss ch-sp of prev rnd, tr into 7sts* rep from * to * 9 times, ch1, ss into 3rd of starting ch3

Round 8: ch3, tr into base of ch3 (counts as first 2tr inc), tr into 5sts, 2tr inc, *ch1, miss ch-sp of prev rnd, 2tr inc, 5tr, 2tr inc* rep from * to * 9 times, ch1, ss into 3rd of starting ch3

Round 9: ch3 (counts as first tr), tr into 8sts, *ch1, miss ch-sp of prev rnd, tr into 9sts* rep from * to * 9 times, ch1, ss into 3rd of starting ch3

Round 10: ch3 (counts as first tr), tr into 8sts, *†ch1, tr into ch-sp, ch1†, tr into 9sts* rep from * to * 9 times, rep from † to † once more, ss into 3rd of starting ch3

Round 11: ch2, tr into next st (counts as first tr2tog), *†tr into 5sts, tr2tog, ch2, [tr into ch-sp, ch2] twice†, tr2tog* rep from * to * 9 times, rep from † to † once more, ss into top of first tr

Round 12: ch2, tr into next st (counts as first tr2tog), *†tr into 3sts, tr2tog, ch2, [tr into ch-sp, ch2] 3 times†, tr2tog* rep from * to * 9 times, rep from † to † once more, ss into top of first tr

Round 13: ch2, tr into next st (counts as first tr2tog), *†tr, tr2tog, ch2, [tr into next ch-sp, ch2] 4 times†, tr2tog* rep from * to * 9 times, rep from † to † once more, ss into top of first tr

Round 14: ch2, tr2tog (counts as first tr3tog), *†ch2, [tr into next ch-sp, ch2] 5 times†, tr3tog* rep from * to * 9 times, rep from † to † once more, ss into top of first tr2tog, fasten off

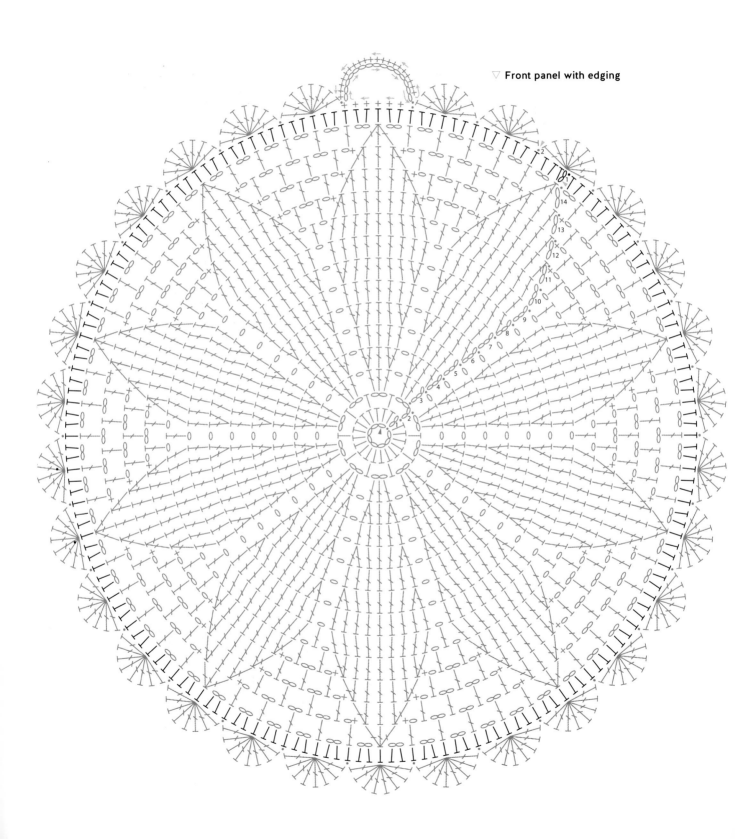

▽ **Front panel with edging**

▷ FRONT PANEL

This panel is joined to the back panel by sewing the two pieces together at the centre, then joining as you go with joining dc (jdc) sts in rounds 11 to 13.

First: leaving a 30cm (12in) tail of yarn at the beginning, work as given for back panel to the end of rnd 10

Next: lay the back and front panels together, with WS facing, and line up the stitch pattern at the centre. Whip stitch through the centre hole and htr sts of rnd 1; fasten off yarn between the two panels and weave in the loose end

Round 11: line up the petals of the daisy motif and continue with ch3, tr into next st (counts as first tr2tog), *†tr into 5sts, tr2tog, jdc into corresponding ch-sp on rnd 11 of back panel, ch1, tr into ch-sp, ch2, tr into next ch-sp, ch1, jdc†, tr2tog* rep from * to * 9 times, rep from † to † once more, ss into top of first tr

Round 12: ch3, tr into next st (counts as first tr2tog), *†tr into 3sts, tr2tog, jdc, ch1, [tr into ch-sp, ch2] twice, tr into next ch-sp, ch1, jdc†, tr2tog* rep from * to * 9 times, rep from † to † once more, ss into top of first tr

Round 13: ch3, tr into next st (counts as first tr2tog), *†tr into next st, tr2tog, jdc, ch1, [tr into ch-sp, ch2] 3 times, tr into next ch-sp, ch1, jdc †, tr2tog* rep from * to * 9 times, rep from † to † once more, ss into top of first tr

Round 14: work as given for back panel, fasten off

▷ EDGING

All of the sts in rnd 1 of the edging are worked through corresponding sts and ch-sps of both back and front panels together.

Round 1: with front panel facing join yarn B in the top of any tr3tog st (of both back and front panels), ch2, htr into base of ch2, [2htr into ch-sp, htr into next st] 59 times, 2htr into ch-sp, ss into 1st htr (180sts), fasten off

Round 2: join yarn C in 4th htr st of prev rnd, *miss 2sts, 8tr scallop into next st, miss 2sts, ss into next st* rep from * to * twice

Hanging loop: dc into 6sts, ch15, working backwards ss into same space as prev ss, working forwards 20dc into ch-sp, ss into same space as 6th dc

Continue round 2: *miss 2sts, 8tr scallop into next st, miss 2sts, ss into next st* rep from * to * 27 times (29 scallops + 1 hanging loop), fasten off and weave in loose ends

▷ BLOCKING

Using a press cloth, steam press on reverse with a hot iron.

VINTAGE FOLK MEDALLION POTHOLDER

Where would crochet be if it weren't for the rise of granny chic? It is hardly worth thinking about! If, like me, you are a huge fan of this style trend, then this potholder is a must for your crochet make list as no potholder wall will be complete without it. Its gorgeous colour combination of emerald, orange and sunny yellow with just a hint of pretty pink and blue is vintage folk style, and epitomizes all that we love about granny chic.

▽ Front panel with edging

Tools and Materials

▸ Size 3mm (US C2 or D3) crochet hook

▸ 100g balls (280m/306yd) of DMC Petra, size 3, one each in shades 54463/Sky (yarn A), 5722/Orange (yarn B), 53814/Emerald (yarn C), 5742/Yellow (yarn D), 54461/Pale Pink (yarn E) and B5200/White (yarn F)

▸ Yarn needle

▸ Scissors

Yarn Substitution

Any standard 4ply (fingering) weight cotton yarn can easily be substituted for the stated yarn; however, substituting the stated yarn may alter the yarn amounts required and the finished size.

Special Stitches

5tr-fpcl = five treble front post cluster

Tension (Gauge)

7 rnds in tr sts (12st increase each rnd) = 10cm (4in)

Finished Size

16.5cm (6½in) from edge to edge

22cm (8¾in) from point to point

PATTERN

▷ FRONT PANEL

Foundation ring: using yarn A and 3mm hook, leave a 30cm (12in) tail of yarn, ch6, ss to form ring

Round 1: ch3 (counts as first tr), 13tr into ring, ss into 3rd of starting ch3

Round 2: ss between ch3 and first tr of prev rnd, ch4 (counts as first tr, ch1), *†[2tr shell, ch1] between next 2sts†, [tr, ch1] between next 2sts* rep from * to * 6 times, rep from † to † once more, ss into 3rd of starting ch4, fasten off

Round 3: join yarn B between sts of any 2tr shell of prev rnd, ch5 (counts as first tr, ch2), *†5tr-fpcl onto tr, ch2†, tr between sts of 2tr shell, ch2* rep from * to * 6 times, rep from † to † once more, ss into 3rd of starting ch5

Round 4: ss into next ch-sp, ch4 (counts as first tr, ch1), [tr, ch1] twice into same ch-sp, [tr, ch1] 3 times into each ch-sp around, ss into 3rd of starting ch4, fasten off

Round 5: join yarn C between 'tr, ch1' repeats of prev rnd, ch4 (counts as first tr, ch1), *†miss tr of prev rnd, 5tr-fpcl onto next tr, ch1†, miss tr of prev rnd, [tr, ch1] into next ch-sp* rep from * to * 13 times, rep from † to † once more, ss into 3rd of starting ch4, fasten off

Round 6: join yarn A in any ch-sp, ch3 (counts as first tr), 2tr into same ch-sp, 3tr shell into each ch-sp around, ss into 3rd of starting ch3, fasten off

Round 7: join yarn E in same space as ss of prev rnd, ch1, dc into base of ch1, dc into 11sts, *†htr into 2sts, miss 1 st of prev rnd, tr, 3dtr inc, tr, miss 1 st of prev rnd, htr into 2sts†, dc into 12sts * rep from * to * 3 times, rep from † to † once more, ss into first dc

Round 8: ch2 (counts as first htr), htr, dc into 8sts, htr into 3sts, tr into 3sts, *†[2tr, ch1, 2tr] into next st†, tr into 3sts, htr into 3sts, dc into 8sts, htr into 3sts, tr into 3sts* rep from * to * 3 times, rep from † to † once more, tr into 3sts, htr, ss into 2nd of starting ch2

Round 9: ch3 (counts as first tr), tr into 17sts, *†[2tr, ch1, 2tr] into corner ch-sp, miss 1 st of prev rnd†, tr into 23sts* rep from * to * 3 times, rep from † to † once more, tr into 5sts, fasten off invisibly

Round 10: join yarn F in any corner ch-sp, ch3, *†miss 3sts of prev rnd, 3tr shell into next st, [miss 2sts, 3tr shell into next st] 7 times†, [3tr, ch1, 3tr] into corner ch-sp* rep from * to * 3 times, rep from † to † once more, [3tr, ch1, 2tr] into last corner ch-sp, ss into 3rd of starting ch3

Rounds 11–13: rnd 10 sets the pattern for a traditional granny square design, continue in this way working 3tr shells between those of the prev rnd and [3tr, ch1, 3tr] into each corner, fasten off invisibly

▷ BACK PANEL

Foundation ring: using 3mm hook and yarn A, ch6, ss to form ring

Round 1: ch3 (counts as first tr), 13tr into ring, ss into 3rd of starting ch3 (14sts), fasten off

Round 2: join yarn B in any st, ch4 (counts as first tr, ch1), *†[tr, ch1] twice into next st†, [tr, ch1] into next st* rep from * to * 6 times, rep from † to † once more, ss into 3rd of starting ch4 (21sts)

Round 3: ss into next ch-sp, ch3 (counts as first tr), tr into same ch-sp, 2tr inc into each ch-sp around, ss into 3rd of starting ch3 (42sts), fasten off

Round 4: join yarn C in any st, ch3 (counts as first tr), tr into each st around, ss into 3rd of starting ch3 (42sts), fasten off

Round 5: join yarn D in any st, ch3 (counts as first tr), tr into base of ch3, 2tr inc into each st around, ss into 3rd of starting ch3 (84sts), fasten off

Round 6: work as given for rnd 7 of front panel

Round 7: work as given for rnd 8 of front panel

Round 8: work as given for rnd 9 of front panel

Round 9: work as given for rnd 10 of front panel

Round 10: work as given for rnd 11 of front panel

Round 11: work as given for rnd 12 of front panel

Round 12: work as given for rnd 13 of front panel

▽ **Back panel**

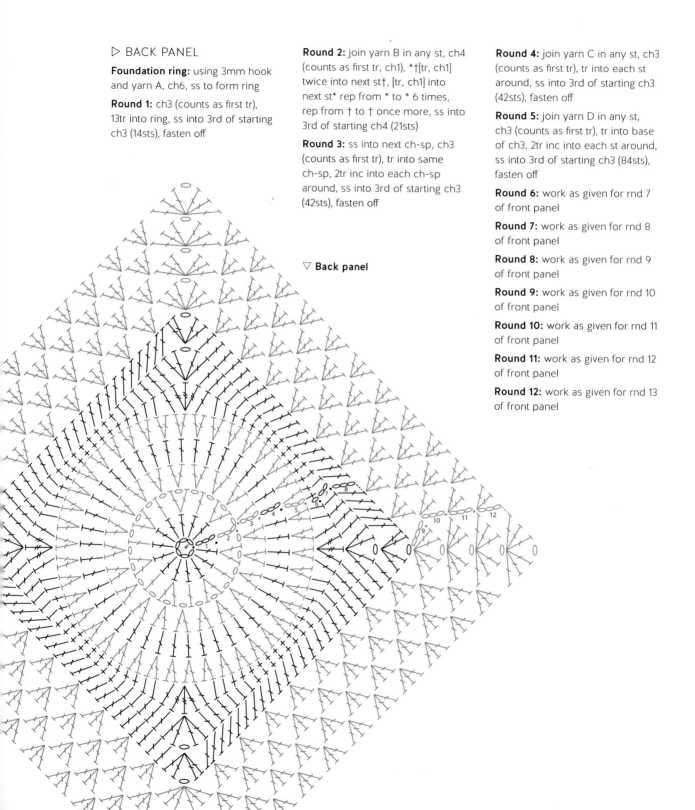

△ Front panel

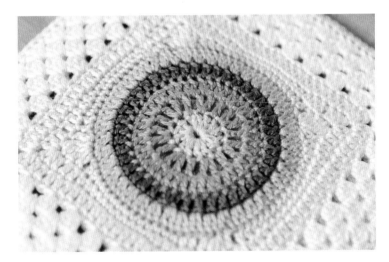

Back panel ▽

TIPS AND TRICKS

In crochet, turning a circular motif into a square one (squaring a circle) can sometimes be tricky, especially as your tension can influence the outcome greatly. If your potholder begins to cup or ripple a little when working rounds 7 to 9, it's likely that the blocking process will resolve the issue. However, if it begins to resemble a bowl or becomes too floppy, re-check your tension and adjust your hook size accordingly.

▷ MAKING UP

Join Front and Back Panels

Weave in loose ends of front and back panels. Lay front and back panels together, with WS facing, and line up the stitch pattern. Using the yarn needle and 30cm (12in) tail of yarn, sew the two panels together using a whip stitch through the centre hole and sts of rnd 1; fasten off yarn between the two panels and weave in the loose end.

Edging

All of the edging sts are worked through corresponding sts and ch-sps of both front and back panels together.

Round 1: join yarn A in any corner ch-sp, ch1, dc into 39sts along the side, 3dc into corner ch-sp, dc into 3sts

Hanging loop: ch15, working backwards ss into 8th st, ss into 9th st, working forwards 20dc into ch-sp, ss into same space as last dc before 15ch

Continue round 1: dc into 36sts, *†3dc into corner ch-sp†, dc into 39sts* rep from * to * twice, rep from † to † once more, fasten off invisibly and weave in loose ends

▷ BLOCKING

Using a press cloth, steam press on reverse with a hot iron.

OCTO-POP POTHOLDER

The chunkier the potholder the more practical it is to use around your kitchen. Whether protecting delicate hands when carrying warm pans or protecting your work surfaces from direct heat, this potholder with its densely packed, nubby popcorn stitches is most definitely up to the task, and it looks very pretty, too!

▽ Front panel
with edging

Tools and Materials

▸ Size 3mm (US C2 or D3) crochet hook

▸ 100g balls (280m/306yd) of DMC Petra, size 3, one each in shades 54463/Sky (yarn A), B5200/White (yarn B) and 5742/Yellow (yarn C)

▸ Yarn needle

▸ Scissors

Yarn Substitution

Any standard 4ply (fingering) weight cotton yarn can easily be substituted for the stated yarn; however, checking your tension carefully beforehand is strongly recommended.

Special Stitches

pc = popcorn stitch

In this pattern popcorn stitches are worked using 7 treble stitches, and chain stitches worked afterwards are not counted as part of the popcorn stitch.

Tension (Gauge)

7 rnds in tr sts (12st increase each rnd) = 10cm (4in)

Finished Size

18cm (7in) diameter (excluding hanging loop)

PATTERN

▷ FRONT PANEL

Foundation ring: using 3mm hook and yarn A, leave a 30cm (12in) tail of yarn, ch5, ss to form ring

Round 1: ch4 (counts as first tr, ch1), [tr, ch1] 7 times into ring, ss into 3rd of starting ch4

Round 2: ss into ch-sp, ch2, [pc, ch2] into each ch-sp around, ss into top of 1st pc (8pc)

Round 3: ss into next ch-sp, ch2, [pc, ch2, pc, ch1] into each ch-sp around, ss into top of 1st pc (16pc)

Round 4: ss into next ch-sp, ch3 (counts as first tr), [tr, ch1, 2tr] into same ch-sp, *tr into next (side) ch-sp, [2tr, ch1, 2tr] into next (corner) ch-sp* rep from * to * 7 times, tr into (side) ch-sp, ss into 3rd of starting ch3

Round 5: ch3 (counts as first tr), *†[2tr, ch1, 2tr] into corner ch-sp†, tr into 2 side sps (between sts of prev rnd)* rep from * to * 7 times, rep from † to † once more, tr into side sp, ss into 3rd of starting ch3

Round 6: ss into side sp, ch3 (counts as first tr), *†[2tr, ch1, 2tr] into corner ch-sp, [tr, ch1] into side sp, [pc, ch1] into next side sp†, tr into side sp* rep from * to * 7 times, rep from † to † once more, ss into 3rd of starting ch3

Round 7: ss into next side sp, ch3 (counts as first tr), *†[2tr, ch1, 2tr] into corner ch-sp, tr into 4 side sps* rep from * to * 7 times, rep from † to † once more, tr into 3 side sps, ss into 3rd of starting ch3

Round 8: work as given for rnd 7 and crochet 5 tr sts along each side

Round 9: work as given for rnd 7 and crochet 6 tr sts along each side

Round 10: ss into next side sp, ch3 (counts as first tr), *†[2tr, ch1, 2tr] into corner ch-sp, tr into 3 side sps, ch1, [pc, ch1] into next side sp†, tr into 3 side sps* rep from * to * 7 times, rep from † to † once more, tr into 2 side sps, ss into 3rd of starting ch3

Round 11: ss into next side sp, ch3 (counts as first tr), *†[2tr, ch1, 2tr] into corner ch-sp, tr into 3 side sps, ch1, [pc, ch1] into 2 ch-sps†, tr into 3 side sps* rep from * to * 7 times, rep from † to † once more, tr into 2 side sps, ss into 3rd of starting ch3

Round 12: work as given for rnd 11 and crochet [pc, ch1] into 3 ch-sps along each side

Round 13: work as given for rnd 11 and crochet [pc, ch1] into 4 ch-sps along each side, fasten off invisibly

▷ BACK PANEL

Foundation ring: using yarn A and 3mm hook, ch5, ss to form ring

Round 1: ch4 (counts as first tr, ch1), [tr, ch1] 7 times into ring, ss into 3rd of starting ch4

Round 2: ss into next ch-sp, ch3 (counts as first tr), [tr, ch1] into same ch-sp, [2tr, ch1] into each ch-sp around, ss into 3rd of starting ch3

Round 3: ch3 (counts as first tr), [2tr, ch1, 2tr] into 7 ch-sps, [2tr, ch1, tr] into last ch-sp, ss into 3rd of starting ch3

Round 4: ss into sp between ch3 and first tr st of prev rnd, ch3 (counts as first tr), *†[2tr, ch1, 2tr] into corner ch-sp†, tr into side sp (between corner sts of prev rnd)* rep from * to * 7 times, rep from † to † once more, ss into 3rd of starting ch3

Round 5: ss into next side sp (between ch3 and first tr of prev rnd), ch3 (counts as first tr), *†[2tr, ch1, 2tr] into corner ch-sp†, tr into 2 side sps* rep from * to * 7 times, rep from † to † once more, tr into side sp, ss into 3rd of starting ch3

Rounds 6–13: the pattern for the basic octagon motif is now set, continue as given for rnd 5 and increase the number of tr sts along each side by 1 for each new rnd, fasten off invisibly

▷ MAKING UP

Join Front and Back Panels

Lay the front and back panels together, with WS facing, and line up the stitch pattern at the centre. Using the yarn needle and 30cm (12in) tail of yarn, sew the two panels together using a whip stitch through the centre hole and tr sts of rnd 1, fasten off between the two panels and weave in the loose end.

Edging

All of the sts in rnd 1 of the edging are worked through corresponding sts and ch-sps of both front and back panels together.

Round 1: with front panel facing, join yarn B in any corner ch-sp (of both front and back panels), ch2 (counts as first htr), *htr into 5 tr sts, htr into 4 pc sts (working through centre of each pc st),

htr into 5 tr sts, [htr, ch2, htr] into corner ch-sp* rep from * to * 7 times, rep from to once more, [htr, ch2] into last corner ch-sp, ss into top of 1st htr, fasten off

Round 2: join yarn C in any corner ch-sp, ch1, miss 1st of prev rnd, dc into 14sts, ch15, miss [1st, ch-sp, 2sts] of prev rnd, dc into 14sts, *3dc into corner ch-sp, miss 1st of prev rnd, dc into 15sts* rep from * to * 6 times, 3dc into corner ch-sp, ss into first dc

Round 3: ch1, dc into base of ch1, dc into 13sts, 20dc into ch-sp, dc into 15sts, *†2dc inc into corner st†, dc into 17sts* rep from * to * 6 times, rep from † to † once more, dc into next st, fasten off invisibly and weave in loose ends

▷ BLOCKING

To avoid crushing the popcorn stitches, steam block only; **do not** press.

TINY SQUARES PATCHWORK CUSHION

This design was originally inspired by my appreciation of vintage quilt designs, particularly postage stamp quilts made from small squares of fabric. I love how even the simplest design can lend itself to a vast array of interpretations and colour arrangements, although I have always been particularly fond of this classic chequerboard pattern.

Tools and Materials

- Size 3.5mm (US E4) crochet hook
- 50g balls (135m/148yd) of Rowan Baby Merino Silk, two in shade 670/Snowdrop (yarn A), three in shade 674/Shell Pink (yarn B), one each in shades 688/Sunshine (yarn C), 692/Leaf (yarn D), 687/Strawberry (yarn E), 694/Frosty (yarn F), 672/Dawn (yarn G) and 696/Lake (yarn H)
- Five 1.5cm (⅝in) shank buttons
- 40 x 30cm (16 x 12in) cushion
- Yarn needle
- Scissors
- Pins
- Sewing needle and thread to coordinate with yarn B

Tension (Gauge)

Each tiny square motif should measure approx. 4cm (1½in) across

21sts and 12 rows in rows of tr sts = 10cm (4in)

Finished Size

40 x 30cm (16 x 12in)

PATTERN

▷ FRONT PANEL

Crochet Tiny Square Motifs

Make 40 in yarn A; 8 in yarn B; 7 each in yarns C and D; 5 each in yarns E and F; 4 each in yarns G and H.

Foundation ring: using yarn and 3.5mm hook, ch6, ss to form ring

Round 1: ch4 (counts as first tr, ch1), [4tr, ch1] 3 times into ring, 3tr into ring, ss to 3rd of starting ch4

Round 2: ch3 (counts as first tr), *†[2tr, ch1, 2tr] into corner ch-sp, miss 1 st of prev rnd†, tr into 3sts* rep from * to * 3 times, rep from † to † once more, tr into 2sts, fasten off invisibly

Join Tiny Square Motifs

Arrange the tiny square motifs face up in an 8 x 11 grid, matching the arrangement shown in the colour placement diagram to create a chequerboard design.

Using yarn A, join the motifs from the back, working in rows of dc stitches vertically then horizontally. Crochet 1 dc into each corner ch-sp and 1 dc into the top of each side st. When working the horizontal joining rows, simply crochet over the top of the vertical rows when you come to them.

▷ BACK PANEL

The back panel is worked in two sections that are crocheted directly onto the front panel along the short ends as follows:

Section 1

Row 1: along first short end of the front panel, with RS facing, join yarn B in the top rightmost corner ch-sp of first tiny square motif, ch2, tr into same space, *†tr into 7 sts†, tr2tog over next two corner ch-sps (1st + 2nd motifs)* rep from * to * 7 times, rep from † to † once more, tr into last corner ch-sp (65sts), **turn**

Row 2: ch2, tr into 7sts, *tr2tog, tr into 6sts* rep from * to * 6 times, tr2tog, tr into 8 sts (58sts), **turn**

Row 3: ch2, tr into 58sts, **turn**

Rows 4–8: rep row 3

Row 9: with RS facing, join yarn E in rightmost st of prev row, ch1, dc into 58sts, **turn**

Row 10: ch1, dc into 58sts, **turn**

Row 11: ch1, dc into 8sts, *ch2, miss 1st of prev row, dc into 9sts* rep from * to * 5 times, **turn**

Row 12: ch1, *dc into 9sts, 2dc into ch-sp* rep from * to * 5 times, dc into 8sts, fasten off

Row 13: with RS facing join yarn C in rightmost st of prev row, ch1, dc into 63sts, fasten off

Section 2

Rows 1–3: on the other short end of the front panel work as given for rows 1-3 of section 1

Rows 4–30: rep row 3 of section 1

Row 31: ch1, dc into 58sts, **turn**

Row 32–34: rep row 31, fasten off

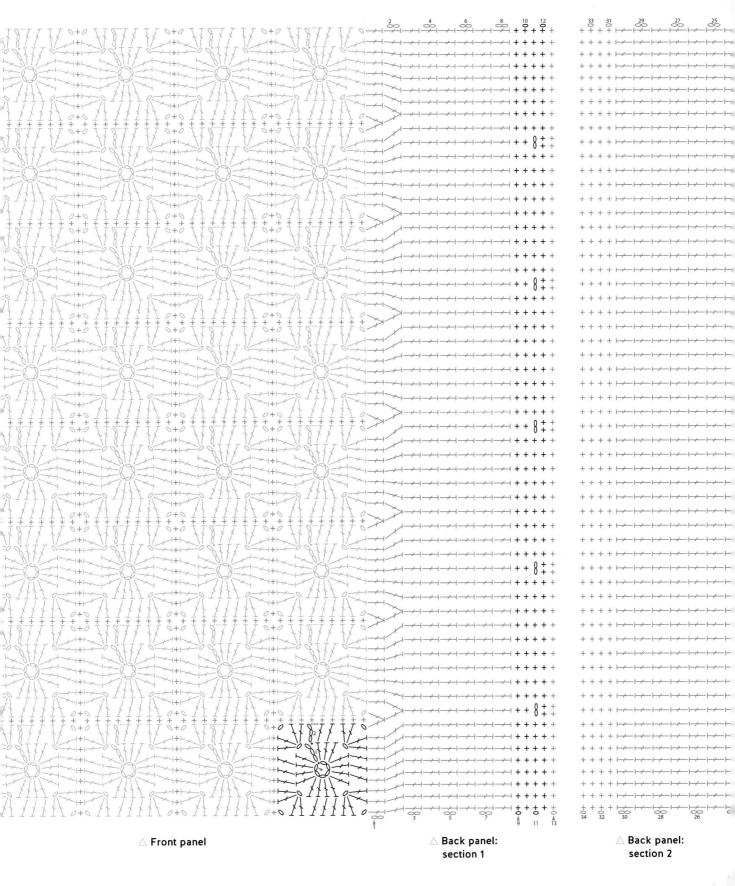

△ Front panel

△ Back panel:
section 1

△ Back panel:
section 2

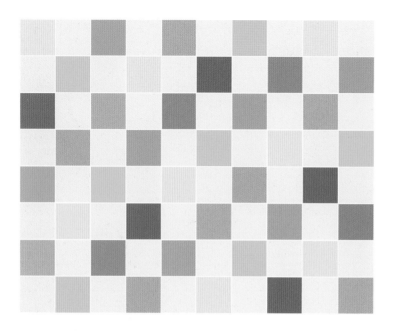

COLOUR PLACEMENT

▷ Snowdrop
▷ Shell Pink
▶ Sunshine
▶ Leaf
▶ Strawberry
▶ Frosty
▶ Dawn
▶ Lake

▷ BLOCKING

The front panel is larger than the back panel, so that when the cushion cover is complete the front panel will wrap around the cushion insert more than in a standard cushion design.

Steam block the front panel to 42 x 32cm (16½ x 13in).

Steam block section 1 of the back panel to 28cm (11in) square and section 2 to 10 x 28cm (4 x 11in).

▷ MAKING UP

Join Side Seams

All side seam sts are worked through corresponding sts and ch-sps of both front panel and back panel sections together.

First: fold section 2 of the back panel onto the front panel with WS facing, and pin in place along the sides, lining it up with 8 of the tiny square motifs of the front panel

Next: fold section 1 of the back panel and pin in place along the sides, lining it up with the remaining 2 tiny square motifs of the front panel and with the contrasting button band overlapping section 2

Next: with RS of cushion facing, join yarn A in corner ch-sp of top rightmost tiny square motif and ch1

Next: work a row of dc sts along the side of the cushion, working into each ch-sp and 8sts of tiny square motifs, joining them to corresponding tr and dc sts of back panel (note that you will work into each tr st twice, the stem and the top of the st) working through three layers at the button band overlap, fasten off

Next: rep for second side seam, fasten off and weave in loose ends

Add Buttons

On row 32 (2nd row of dc sts) of section 2 of the back panel mark 9th, 19th, 29th, 39th and 49th sts with a pin. Sew a button onto each of the marked sts with the sewing needle and thread.

 TIPS AND TRICKS

A great stash-busting project for those precious leftovers that you can't bear to part with. Each tiny square motif uses approx. 4m (4⅜yd) of yarn, and if you can find 40 different colours in your stash, one for each tiny coloured square, you will be able to crochet a truly unique cushion cover.

PINWHEEL PATCHWORK & LOG CABIN CUSHIONS

Many of my crochet designs are inspired by my love of vintage quilts and the triangle square motifs in the Pinwheel Patchwork Cushion have been combined to emulate a pinwheel quilt block, while in the Log Cabin Cushion the design elaborates on this basic motif with well-placed colour changes to give the effect of a log cabin quilt block. I have chosen a custom-dyed yarn, Blissful Plump from the Skein Queen, each colour expertly hand-dyed to match one of my favourite palettes of the moment, intense sapphire blue with coral, soft peach, mint and amethyst.

PINWHEEL PATCHWORK CUSHION

Tools and Materials

- Size 4mm (US G6) crochet hook
- 100g (224m/245yd) skeins Skein Queen Blissful Plump (100% Blue Faced Leicester), two in shade Sapphire (yarn A) and one each in shades Naked (yarn B), Coraline (yarn C), Peachy Cream (yarn D), Mint Julep (yarn E) and Parma Violets (yarn F)
- Five 2cm (¾in) buttons
- 40cm (16in) square cushion
- Stitch holders (small safety pins or scrap yarn)
- Yarn needle
- Scissors
- Pins
- Sewing needle and thread to coordinate with yarn B

Yarn Substitution

Any standard DK (light worsted) weight yarn can easily be substituted for the stated yarn; however, checking your tension carefully beforehand is strongly recommended.

Tension (Gauge)

Each triangle square motif should measure 7.5cm (3in) square

5 rnds of granny square motif worked in tr sts = 10cm (4in)

Finished Size

40cm (16in) square

TIPS AND TRICKS

Crochet the triangle square motif in two halves: the first section in one colour where the work is turned at the end of each round; then crochet the second section onto the first. Join at the beginning and end of each round with slip stitches and half treble stitches. It is important that these joining stitches are worked into the correct place of the first section of the motif so that the stitches and motif lie neatly. For step-by-step guidance, see **Techniques**.

PATTERN

▷ FRONT PANEL

Triangle Square Motif – First Section

Make 25.

Foundation ring: using yarn B and 4mm hook, ch6, ss to form ring

Round 1 (RS): ch3 (counts as first tr), 2tr, ch2, 3tr, ch1, **turn**

Round 2: ch3 (counts as first tr), tr into 4th ch from hook, tr into 2sts, miss 1st of prev rnd, [2tr, ch2, 2tr] into corner ch-sp, tr into 2sts, f2tr inc into 3rd of ch3 of prev rnd, ch1, **turn**

Round 3: ch3 (counts as first tr), tr into 4th ch from hook, tr into 5sts, miss 1st of prev rnd, [2tr, ch2, 2tr] into corner ch-sp, tr into 5sts, f2tr inc into 3rd of ch3 of prev rnd, ch1, **turn**

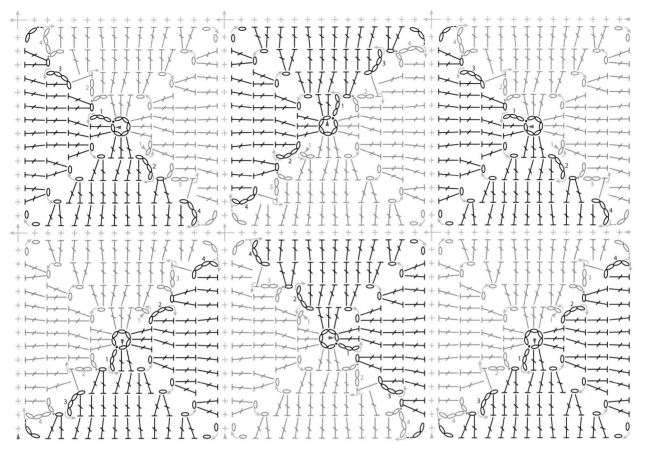

Round 4: ch3 (counts as first tr), tr into 4th ch from hook, tr into 8sts, miss 1st of prev rnd, [2tr, ch2, 2tr] into corner ch-sp, tr into 8sts, f2tr inc into 3rd of ch3 of prev rnd, ch2, slip working loop onto a stitch holder and cut a 15cm (6in) tail of yarn

Triangle Square Motif – Second Section

Make 5 each in yarns A, C, D, E and F. Refer to **Techniques** for step-by-step demonstration of where the beginning and end stitches of each round are worked into the first section of the triangle square motif.

Round 1: with RS facing, join yarn in ch st at the end of rnd 1 of first section, ch2, [3tr, ch2, 3tr] into foundation ring of first section, ch2, ss into f2tr inc of rnd 2 of first section

Round 2: ch2, htr into ch st at the end of rnd 2 of first section, **turn**, tr into ch-sp of prev rnd, tr into 2sts, miss 1st of prev rnd, [2tr, ch2, 2tr] into corner ch-sp, tr into 2sts, miss 1st of prev rnd, 2tr into ch-sp, ch2, ss into f2tr inc of rnd 3 of first section

Round 3: ch2, htr into ch st at the end of rnd 3, **turn**, tr into ch-sp of prev rnd, tr into 5sts, miss 1st of prev rnd, [2tr, ch2, 2tr] into corner ch-sp, tr into 5sts, 2tr into next sp (created by htr of prev rnd), ch2, ss into f2tr inc of rnd 4 of first section, **turn**

Round 4: ch3 (counts as first tr), tr into ch-sp, tr into 8sts, miss 1st of prev rnd, [2tr, ch2, 2tr] into corner ch-sp, tr into 8sts, 2tr into next sp (created by htr of prev rnd), ch2, fasten off invisibly to 3rd of starting ch3 of rnd 4 of first section

Finish Triangle Square Motif

Next: using yarn needle, pick up tail of yarn from end of first section and fasten off invisibly to 3rd of starting ch3 of rnd 4 of second section

Join Triangle Square Motifs

Arrange the triangle square motifs face up in a 5 x 5 grid matching the arrangement shown in the colour placement diagram to create a pinwheel design.

Using yarn A, join the motifs from the back, working rows of dc stitches vertically then horizontally. Crochet 1 dc into each corner ch-sp and 1 dc into the top of each side st.

Note that due to the construction technique of the triangle square motif, where the colour change is in the corner of the motif, either the first or last joining sts (excluding the corner sts) should be worked through the corner ch-sp and first or last side st. This will become apparent when working the rows of joining sts.

Edging and Button Flap

Side 1: along any side of the front panel, join yarn A in 7th st from corner of left most triangle square motif, ch1, dc into base of ch1, dc into 6sts, [dc, ch2, dc] into corner ch-sp

Side 2: *dc into 11sts, dc into ch-sp, dc2tog over same and next ch-sp, dc into 12sts, dc2tog over next 2 ch-sps* rep from * to * twice, dc into 11sts, [2dc, ch2, dc] into corner ch-sp

Side 3: *†dc into 12sts, dc2tog over next 2 ch-sps, dc into 11sts, dc into ch-sp, dc2tog over same and next ch-sp* rep from * to * twice†, dc into 12sts, [dc, ch2, dc] into corner ch-sp

Side 4: rep side 2

Side 1: rep from † to † of side 3, dc into 5sts, ss into first dc, **turn**

Button flap row 1: ch1, dc into front loop of 50sts, **turn**

Rows 2–5: ch1, dc into 50sts, fasten off

▷ BACK PANEL

The back panel of this cushion is a one colour, basic granny square crocheted as follows:

Foundation ring: using yarn A and 4mm hook, ch6, ss to form ring

Round 1: s-tr, [2tr, ch2] into ring, [3tr, ch2] - 3 times into ring, ss into top of s-tr

Round 2: s-tr, [3tr, ch2, 3tr] into next 3 ch-sps, [3tr, ch2, 2tr] into last ch-sp, ss into top of s-tr

Round 3: ss into side sp (between ch3 and first tr of prev rnd), s-tr, 2tr into same sp, *†[3tr, ch2, 3tr] into corner ch-sp†, 3tr shell into side sp* rep from * to * 3 times, rep from † to † once more, ss into top of s-tr

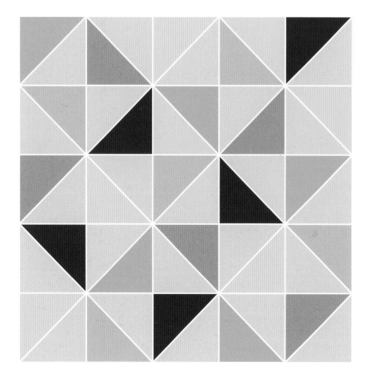

COLOUR PLACEMENT

▷ Naked
▷ Parma Violets
▷ Coraline
▷ Sapphire
▷ Mint Julep
▷ Peachy Cream

Round 4: s-tr, 3tr shell into next side sp, *†[3tr, ch2, 3tr] into corner ch-sp†, 3tr shell into 2 side sps* rep from * to * 3 times, rep from † to † once more, 2tr into last side sp, ss into top of s-tr

Round 5: ss into side sp, s-tr, 2tr into same sp, 3tr shell into next side sp, *†[3tr, ch2, 3tr] into corner ch-sp†, 3tr shell into 3 side sps* rep from * to * 3 times, rep from † to † once more, 3tr shell into side sp, ss into top of s-tr

Rounds 6–22: rnds 1 to 5 set the pattern for the basic granny square motif, continue in this way for rnds 6 to 22, fasten off invisibly

▷ BLOCKING

Steam block the front and back panels to 39cm (15½in) square.

▷ MAKING UP

Edging

All edging sts are worked through corresponding sts and ch-sps of both front and back panels together.

First: with WS facing each other, line up front and back panels

Round 1: with front panel facing, join yarn C in top of first st (of both front and back panels) after button flap, ch1, dc into base of ch1, dc into 7sts, *†3dc into corner ch-sp†, dc into 66sts* rep from * to * 3 times, rep from † to † once more, dc into 8sts, dc into front loop of 50sts in front of button flap, ss into first dc

Next: pull working loop through same space just worked ss to back of work, **turn work** and dc into 50sts of back panel, ss into first edging st after button flap, fasten off and weave in loose ends

Add Buttons

On row 3 of the button flap mark 5th, 15th, 25th, 35th and 45th sts with a pin. Sew a button onto each of the marked sts with the sewing needle and thread.

LOG CABIN CUSHION

Tools and Materials

- Size 4mm (US G6) crochet hook
- Leftover yarns from Pinwheel Patchwork Cushion
- Four 1.5cm (⅝in) buttons
- 35cm (14in) square cushion
- Stitch holders (small safety pins or scrap yarn)
- Yarn needle
- Scissors
- Pins
- Sewing needle and thread to coordinate with yarn D

Tension (Gauge)

19sts and 12 rows in rows of tr sts = 10cm (4in)

Finished Size

35cm (14in) square

PATTERN

▷ FRONT & BACK PANELS

The front and back panels are worked in the same pattern in different colours; yarn colours used for the back panel are shown in brackets. Refer to the colour placement diagram for each numbered section of the design.

Inner Section – First section:
Using yarn A (yarn C) and 4mm hook, work as given for triangle square motif: first section (see Pinwheel Patchwork Cushion) for 11 rnds, slip working loop onto a stitch holder and cut a 15cm (6in) tail of yarn.

Second section: with RS facing and using yarn D (yarn E), work as given for triangle square motif: second section (see Pinwheel Patchwork Cushion) for 11 rnds, fasten off invisibly

Next: finish the triangle square motif by fastening off invisibly with tail of yarn from first section

Middle Section –Third Section
Round 12: with RS facing, join yarn C (yarn F) in corner ch-sp of first section (inner section), ch3 (counts as first tr), tr into same sp, miss 1st of prev rnd, tr into 32sts, [2tr, ch2, 2tr] into corner ch-sp, tr into 32sts, [2tr, ch1] into corner ch-sp, **turn**

Round 13: ch3 (counts as first tr), tr into 4th ch from hook, tr into 35sts, miss 1st of prev rnd, [2tr, ch2, 2tr] into corner ch-sp, tr into 35sts, f2tr inc into 3rd of ch3 of prev rnd, ch1, **turn**

Round 14: work as given for rnd 13 with 38 tr sts along each side

Round 15: work as given for last round of triangle square motif with 41 tr sts along each side, slip working loop onto a stitch holder and cut a 15cm (6in) tail of yarn

Middle Section – Fourth Section
Round 12: with RS facing, join yarn E (yarn A) in ch st at the end of rnd 12 of third section, ch2, 2tr into corner ch-sp of rnd 11, miss 1 st of prev rnd, tr into 32sts, [2tr, ch2, 2tr] into corner ch-sp, tr into 32sts, [2tr, ch2] into corner ch-sp, ss into f2tr inc of rnd 13 of third section

Round 13: ch2, htr into ch st at the end of rnd 13, **turn**, tr into ch-sp of prev rnd, tr into 35sts, miss 1st of prev rnd, [2tr, ch2, 2tr] into corner ch-sp, tr into 35sts, miss 1st of prev rnd, 2tr into ch-sp, ch2, ss into f2tr inc of rnd 14 of first section

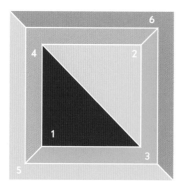

△ Front panel

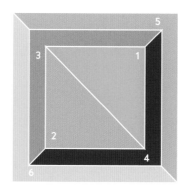

△ Back panel

COLOUR PLACEMENT

▶ Parma Violets
▶ Coraline
▶ Sapphire
▶ Mint Julep
▶ Peachy Cream

Round 14: work as given for rnd 13 with 38 tr sts along each side

Round 15: work as given for last rnd of triangle square motif with 41 tr sts along each side, fasten off invisibly to 3rd of starting ch3 of rnd 15 of third section

Next: finish the triangle square motif by fastening off invisibly with the tail of yarn from the third section

Outer Section – Fifth Section

Rounds 16–19: with RS facing, join yarn D (yarn E) in corner ch-sp of fourth section (middle section) and work as given for third section (middle section)

Outer Section – Sixth Section

Rounds 16–19: join yarn F (yarn D) in ch st at end of rnd 16 of fifth section (middle section) and work as given for fourth section (middle section)

▷ BUTTON FLAP

Row 1: join yarn F in back loop of 9th st from rightmost corner of front panel, ch1, dc into base of ch1, dc into back loop of 40sts, **turn**

Row 2: ch1, dc into 41sts, **turn**

Rows 3–4: rep row 2, fasten off

▷ BLOCKING

Steam block the front and back panels to 34cm (13½in) square.

▷ MAKING UP

Edging

All edging sts are worked through corresponding sts and ch-sps of both front and back sections together.

First: with WS facing each other, line up front and back panels

Round 1: with front panel facing, join yarn C in top of first st (of both front and back panels) after button flap, ch1, dc into base of ch1, dc into 7sts, *3dc into corner ch-sp, dc into 56sts*, 3dc into 2nd corner ch-sp, dc into 57sts, rep from * to * once more, 3dc into corner ch-sp, dc into 8sts, dc into front loop of 41sts in front of button flap, ss into first dc

Next: pull working loop through same space just worked ss to back of work**, **turn work** and dc into 7sts, *†working backwards ch4, miss 2 dc sts, ss into next 2 dc sts, working forwards 5dc into ch-sp, ss into last dc before ch sts†, dc into 10sts* rep from * to * 3 times, rep from to once more, dc into 4sts, ss into first edging st after button flap, fasten off and weave in loose ends

Add Buttons

On row 1 of the button flap mark 6th, 16th, 26th and 36th sts with a pin. Sew a button onto each of the marked sts with the sewing needle and thread.

FABULOUS ROSE CUSHION

Here is a fabulous oversized flower to get your hook into. This time its layers of pretty petals are crocheted in the softest Italian wool and cashmere blend yarn from Gomitoli's. This cushion cover will surely be a favourite to cuddle up against in your cosy reading corner or crocheting nook.

Tools and Materials

- Size 4.5mm (US 7) crochet hook
- 50g balls (107m/117yd) of Gomitoli's Cashmere Lana, three in shade 10000/Natural (yarn A), three in shade 10028/Pink (yarn B) and one each in shades 10012/Paprika (yarn C), 10008/Saffron yellow (yarn D) and 10033/Sky (yarn E)
- Four 2cm (¾in) buttons
- 35cm (14in) square cushion
- Yarn needle
- Scissors
- Pins
- Sewing needle and thread to coordinate with yarn A

Yarn Substitution

Any standard worsted weight yarn can easily be substituted for the stated yarn; however, checking your tension carefully beforehand is strongly recommended.

Special Stitches

bp-htr = back post half treble

sdc = spike double crochet

Tension (Gauge)

5 rnds of granny square motif worked in tr sts = 10cm (4in)

Finished Size

35cm (14in) square

PATTERN

▷ FRONT PANEL

Foundation ring: using yarn A and 4.5mm hook create an adjustable ring and place starting loop on hook

Round 1: ch4 (counts as first tr, ch1), [tr, ch1] 6 times into ring, close ring, ss into 3rd of starting ch4

Round 2: ch1, dc into base of ch1, *2dc into ch-sp, dc into next st* rep from * to * 6 times, 2dc into ch-sp, ss into first dc

Round 3: ch3 (counts as first tr), [tr, ch1, 2tr, ch1] into base of ch3, *miss 2sts of prev rnd, [2tr, ch1] twice into next st* rep from * to * around (6 times), ss into 3rd of starting ch3, fasten off

Round 4: join yarn C in any ch-sp, ch2, 3tr-cl into same ch-sp (counts as first 4tr-cl), ch2, [4tr-cl, ch2] into each ch-sp around, ss into top of first 3tr-cl, fasten off

Round 5: join yarn A in any 4tr-cl st of prev rnd, ch1, dc into base of ch1, *3dc into ch-sp, dc into next st* rep from * to * 13 times, 3dc into ch-sp, ss into top of first dc

Round 6: ch1, dc into base of ch1, *ch4, miss 3sts of prev rnd, dc into next st* rep from * to * 13 times, ch4, ss into first dc

Round 7: ch1, [dc, htr, 4tr, htr, dc] into each ch-sp around, ss into first dc, fasten off

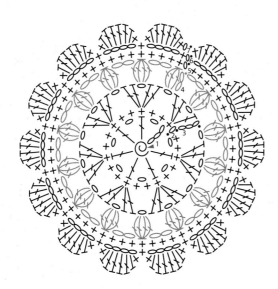

△ **Front panel: centre of rose motif**

Round 8: join yarn D between any 2 dc sts (last and first sts of petals) of prev rnd, ch1, *bp-htr onto dc st of rnd 6, ch5* rep from * to * around, ss into first bp-htr

Round 9: ch1, [dc, htr, tr, 3dtr, tr, htr, dc] into each ch-sp around, ss into first dc, fasten off

Round 10: join yarn E between any 2 dc sts of prev rnd, ch1, *bp-htr onto same st of rnd 8, ch6* rep from * to * around, ss into first bp-htr

Round 11: ch1, [dc, htr, tr, 4dtr, tr, htr, dc] into each ch-sp around, ss into first dc, fasten off

Round 12: join yarn A between any 2 dc sts of prev rnd, ch1, *bp-htr onto same st of rnd 10, ch7* rep from * to * around, ss into first bp-htr

Round 13: ch1, [dc, htr, tr, 5dtr, tr, htr, dc] into each ch-sp around, ss into first dc, fasten off

Round 14: join yarn B between any 2 dc sts of prev rnd and work as given for rnd 12 with bp-htr sts worked onto those of rnd 12

Round 15: work as given for rnd 13, fasten off

Round 16: join yarn C between any 2 dc sts of prev rnd, ch1, *bp-htr onto same st of rnd 14, ch8* rep from * to * around, ss into first bp-htr

Round 17: ch1, [dc, htr, tr, 6dtr, tr, htr, dc] into each ch-sp around, ss into first dc, fasten off

Round 18: join yarn D between any 2 dc sts of prev rnd, ch1, *bp-htr onto same st of rnd 16, ch9* rep from * to * around, ss into first bp-htr

Round 19: ch1, [dc, htr, tr, 7dtr, tr, htr, dc] into each ch-sp around, ss into first dc, fasten off

Round 20: join yarn A between any 2 dc sts of prev rnd and work as given for rnd 18 with bp-htr sts worked onto those of rnd 18

Round 21: ch1, [dc, htr, tr, 8dtr, tr, htr, dc] into each ch-sp around, ss into first dc

▽ **Front panel: petals of rose motif**

Note: Rnds 6 and 7 repeated from previous chart

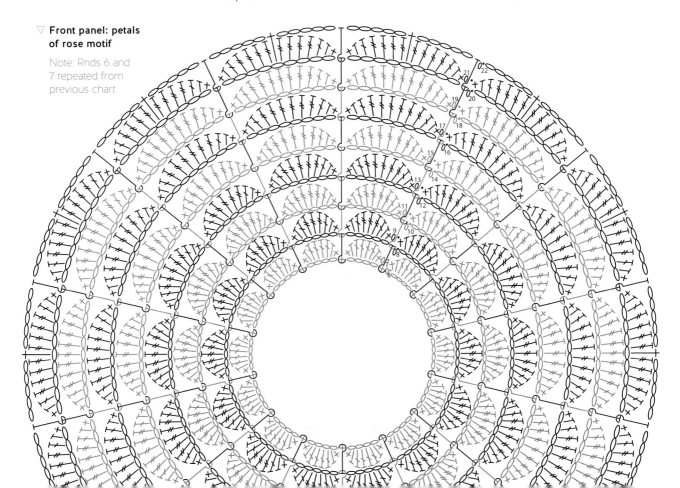

Round 22: ch1, *bp-htr onto same st of rnd 20, ch5, from behind the work dc between 4th and 5th dtr sts of petal of prev rnd onto foundation ch of rnd 20, ch5* rep from * to * around, ss into first bp-htr

Round 23: ch1, *5dc into next 2 ch-sps, 5htr into next ch-sp, [4tr, dtr] into next ch-sp, dtr into next st, [dtr, 4tr] into next ch-sp, 5htr into next ch-sp, 5dc into next ch-sp* rep from * to * 4 times, ss into first dc

Round 24: ch2, htr into base of ch2, htr into 7sts, *†tr into 9sts, dtr into 3sts, [2dtr, ch2, 2dtr] into next st, dtr into 3sts, tr into 9sts†, htr into 11sts* rep from * to * 3 times, rep from † to † once more, htr into 3sts, ss into first htr

Round 25: s-tr, tr into 21sts, *†[2dtr, ch2, 2dtr] into corner ch-sp, miss 1st of prev rnd† tr into 38 sts* rep from * to * around, rep

from † to † once more, tr into 16 sts, ss into top of s-tr

Round 26: s-tr, 2tr into base of s-tr, [miss 2sts of prev rnd, 3tr shell into next st] 7 times, *†[3tr, ch1, 3tr] into corner ch-sp, miss 3sts of prev rnd, 3tr shell into next

st†, [miss 2sts of prev rnd, 3tr shell into next st] 12 times* - rep from * to * 3 times, rep from † to † once more, [miss 2sts of prev rnd, 3tr shell into next st] 4 times, ss into top of s-tr

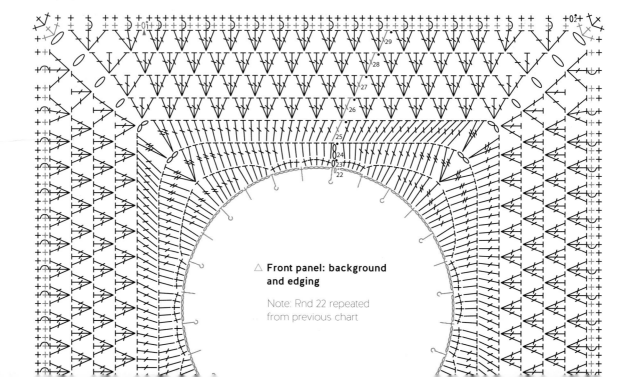

△ **Front panel: background and edging**

Note: Rnd 22 repeated from previous chart

Round 27–29: rnd 26 sets the pattern for a traditional granny square, continue in this way for rnds 27 to 29, fasten off

▷ BUTTON FLAP

Along one side of the front panel, with RS facing, join yarn A in back loop only of 7th st from right-hand corner.

Row 1: ch2, tr into base of ch2, tr into back loop of 41 sts, **turn**

Row 2: ch2, tr into 42sts, **turn**

Row 3: rep row 2, fasten off

▷ BACK PANEL

The back panel of this cushion is a one colour, basic granny square crocheted as follows:

Foundation ring: using yarn B and 4.5mm hook, ch6, ss to form ring

Round 1: s-tr, [2tr, ch1] into ring, [3tr, ch1] 3 times into ring, ss into top of s-tr

Round 2: s-tr, [3tr, ch1, 3tr] into next 3 ch-sps, [3tr, ch1, 2tr] into last ch-sp, ss into top of s-tr

Round 3: ss into side sp (between s-tr and first tr of prev rnd), s-tr, 2tr into same sp, *†[3tr, ch1, 3tr] into corner ch-sp†, 3tr shell into side sp* rep from * to * 3 times, rep from † to † once more, ss into top of s-tr

Round 4: s-tr, 3tr shell into next side sp, *†[3tr, ch1, 3tr] into corner ch-sp†, 3tr shell into 2 side sps* rep from * to * 3 times, rep from † to † once more, 2tr into last side sp, ss into top of s-tr

Round 5: ss into side sp, s-tr, 2tr into same sp, 3tr shell into next side sp, *†[3tr, ch1, 3tr] into corner ch-sp†, 3tr shell into 3 side sps* rep from * to * 3 times, rep from † to † once more, 3tr shell into side sp, ss into top of s-tr

Rounds 6–18: rnds 1–5 set the pattern for the basic granny square motif, continue in this way for rnds 6–18, fasten off

▷ BLOCKING

Steam block the back and front panels to 34cm (13½in) square.

▷ MAKING UP

Edging

All edging sts are worked through corresponding sts and ch-sp of both front and back panels together. Lay panels, with WS facing, lining up the edges and work as follows:

Round 1: with front panel facing, join yarn D in top of first st (of both front and back panels) after button flap, ch1, dc into base of ch1, dc into 5sts, *†3dc into corner ch-sp†, dc into 54sts* rep from * to * 3 times, rep from † to † once more, dc into 6sts, dc into front loop of 42sts in front of button flap, ss into first dc

Next: pull working loop through same sp just worked ss to back of work, turn work and dc into 42sts of back panel, ss into first edging st after button flap, fasten off

Round 2: with front panel facing join yarn A in first st after 3sts of any corner, ch1, dc into base of ch1, *†[sdc into next st, dc into 2sts] 18 times, 3dc into next st†, dc into 2 sts* rep from * to * 3 times (working along the RS of the button flap only), rep from † to † once more, dc into next st, ss into first dc. Fasten off and weave in loose ends

Add Buttons

On row 2 of the button flap mark 8th, 17th, 26th and 35th sts with a pin, then with the sewing needle and thread, sew a button onto each of the marked sts.

CANDY CORN CUSHION

How many times have you splurged out on a gorgeous skein of colourful sock yarn, or beautiful hand-dyed 4ply, only to have it languish at the bottom of your stash basket awaiting the perfect project to make the most of its beauty? If it's more than you care to mention, then this cushion cover might just be the one to finally tempt you into winding one or two of those precious skeins into a ball. The popcorn stitches – an absolute joy to crochet – are so good at making the most of variegated yarns by showing off every colour to maximum effect, and the white background really makes those popcorns pop! I've used a wonderfully soft, pure merino yarn for a cushion cover that feels as good as it looks.

Tools and Materials

- Size 3mm (C2 or D3) crochet hook
- 50g balls (180m/197yd) of Rowan Wool Cotton 4ply, two in shade 483/White (yarn A)
- 100g skeins (400m /437yd) Skein Queen Squash, one each in shades Cupcake Sprinkles (yarn B) and Speckled Elves (yarn C)
- Five 1.5cm (⅝in) buttons
- 35cm (14in) diameter cushion
- Stitch markers (optional)
- Yarn needle
- Scissors
- Pins
- Sewing needle and thread to coordinate with yarn B

Special Stitches

pc = popcorn stitch

In this pattern popcorn stitches are worked using 5 treble stitches followed by 1 chain stitch. Also, in following rounds when working into the top of popcorn stitches, crochet into the first treble stitch and not the chain stitch.

Tension (Gauge)

6 rnds in tr sts (12st increase each rnd) = 10cm (4in)

Finished Size

35cm (14in) diameter

PATTERN

▷ FRONT PANEL

Foundation ring: using yarn and 3mm hook, ch5, ss to form ring

Round 1: s-tr, 11tr into ring, ss into top of s-tr (12sts)

Round 2: s-tr, tr into base of s-tr (counts as first 2tr inc), 2tr inc into each st around, ss into top of s-tr (24sts)

Round 3: s-tr, tr into base of s-tr (counts as first 2tr inc), tr into next st, *2tr inc into next st, tr into next st* rep from * to * around, ss into top of s-tr (36sts)

Round 4: s-tr, tr into base of s-tr (counts as first 2tr inc), tr into 2 sts, *2tr inc into next st, tr into 2 sts* rep from * to * around, ss into top of s-tr (48sts)

Round 5: s-tr, tr into base of s-tr (counts as first 2tr inc), tr into 3 sts, *2tr inc into next st, tr into 3 sts* rep from * to * around, ss into top of s-tr (60sts)

Rounds 6–11: rnds 1 to 5 set the pattern, continue increasing in this way in rnds 6 to 11 (132sts), fasten off

Round 12: join yarn B in first st of any 2tr inc of prev rnd, ch3, tr into base of ch3 (counts as first 2tr inc), *†[pc, tr into 2sts] 3 times, pc†, 2tr inc* rep from * to * 11 times, rep from † to † once more, fasten off invisibly

Round 13: join yarn A in first st of any 2tr inc of prev rnd, ch3, tr into base of ch3 (counts as first 2tr inc), tr into 11sts, *2tr inc into next st, tr into 11sts* rep from * to * around, ss into 3rd of starting ch3 (156sts)

Round 14: s-tr, tr into base of s-tr (counts as first 2tr inc), tr into 12 sts, *2tr inc into next st, tr into 12 sts* rep from * to * around, ss into top of s-tr (168sts), fasten off

Round 15: join yarn C in first st of any 2tr inc of prev rnd, ch3, tr into base of ch3 (counts as first 2tr inc), *†[pc, tr into 2sts] 4 times, pc†, 2tr inc* rep from * to * 11 times, rep from † to † once more, fasten off invisibly

Round 16: join yarn A in first st of any 2tr inc of prev rnd, ch3, tr into base of ch3 (counts as first 2tr inc), tr into 14sts, *2tr inc into next st, tr into 14sts* rep from * to * around (192sts), fasten off invisibly

Round 17: join yarn B in first st of any 2tr inc of prev rnd, ch3 (counts as first tr), tr into next st, *pc, tr into 2sts* rep from * to * around, pc into last st, fasten off invisibly

Round 18: join yarn A in any tr st of prev rnd, ch3 (counts as first tr), tr into each st around (192sts), fasten off invisibly

Round 19: join yarn C in any st of prev rnd, ch3 (counts as first tr), tr into next st, *pc, tr into 2sts* rep from * to * around, pc into last st, fasten off invisibly

Round 20: join yarn B in any pc st of prev rnd and work as given for rnd 19

Round 21: join yarn C in any pc st of prev rnd and work as given for rnd 19

Round 22: rep rnd 20

Round 23: join yarn A in any st, ch3, tr into base of ch3 (counts as first 2tr inc), tr into 15sts, *2tr inc into next st, tr into 15sts* rep from * to * around, ss into 3rd of starting ch3 (204sts)

Round 24: s-tr, tr into each st around, ss into top of s-tr (204sts)

Button Flap

Row 1: ch1, dc into base of ch1, dc into back loop only of 64sts, **turn**

Rows 2–5: ch1, dc into 65sts, **turn**, fasten off

▷ BACK PANEL

Work as given for the front panel to the end of rnd 24.

Buttonhole Section

Row 1: ch1, dc into base of ch1, dc into 9sts, *ch2, miss 1st of prev rnd, dc into 10sts* rep from * to * 5 times, ss into next st, fasten off

▷ BLOCKING

Gently steam block the front and back panels to approx. 34cm (13½in) diameter without over stretching the edges as they should cup to fit the cushion insert.

▷ MAKING UP

Edging

All edging sts are worked through corresponding sts of both the front and back panels together.

First: place the front and back panels together, with WS facing, and line up the button flap and buttonhole section

Next: with the front section facing, join yarn C in first st (of both front and back panels) after button flap, ch1, dc into base of ch1, dc into each st around to the beginning of the button flap, dc into front loop of 65sts in front of button loop, ss into first dc

Next: pull working loop through same space just worked ss to back of work, **turn work** and *dc into 10sts of back panel, 5dc into ch-sp* rep from * to * 5 times, dc into 10sts, ss into first edging st after button flap, fasten off and weave in loose ends

Add Buttons

On row 2 of the button flap, mark 11th, 22nd, 33rd, 44th and 55th sts with a pin. Sew a button onto each of the marked sts with the sewing needle and thread.

TIPS AND TRICKS

If you prefer to keep track of your increases and pattern repeats with stitch markers, place them before each repeat sequence as indicated by the first * in each round of the written pattern. Small safety pins or snippets of contrasting yarns are good alternatives to shop-bought stitch markers.

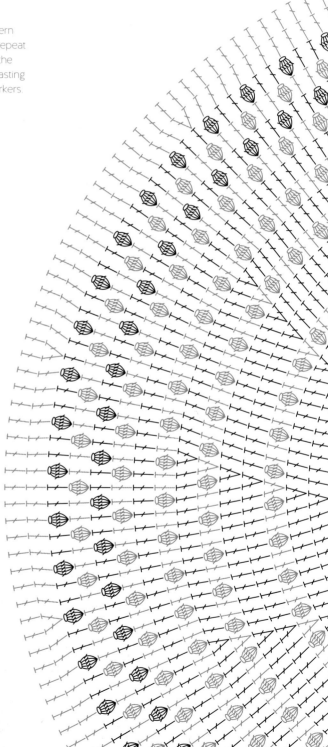

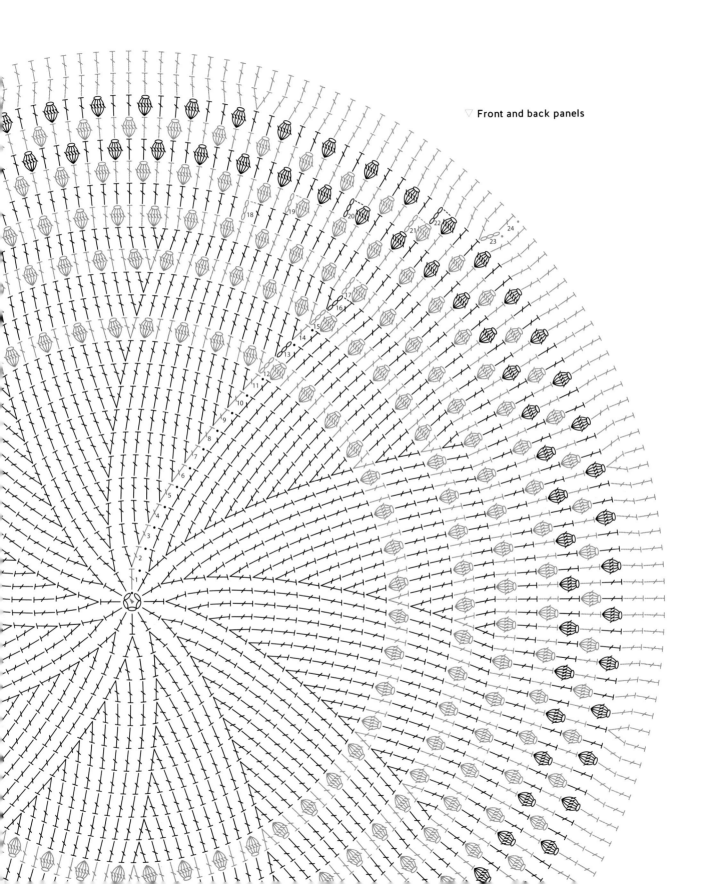

▽ Front and back panels

SCARBOROUGH ROCK FLOOR THROW

I grew up on the north-east coast of England, and when I was a very little girl my family would take day trips to see some of the pretty seaside towns and fishing villages. One I remember well is Scarborough, mostly because of the colourful sticks of 'rock' candy that could be bought there. These long, candy-coloured, sticks of sugary goodness often had the words 'Scarborough Rock' running through the middle of them. Oh, they tasted so good, and the memory of them provided me with the inspiration for this oversized circular throw.

Tools and Materials

- Size 5.5mm (US I9) crochet hook
- 100g skeins (137m/150yd) of Blue Sky Alpacas Worsted Cotton, five in shade 80/Bone (yarn A) and one each in shades 617/Lotus (yarn B), 638/Dandelion (yarn C), 604/Aloe (yarn D), 644/Lavender (yarn E), 642/Pink Parfait (yarn F) and 632/Mediterranean (yarn G)
- Yarn needle
- Scissors

Yarn Substitution

Any standard worsted weight yarn can easily be substituted for the stated yarn; however, checking your tension carefully beforehand is strongly recommended.

Tension (Gauge)

3½ rnds of circular motif worked in tr sts (12st inc each rnd) = 10cm (4in)

Finished Size

Approx. 115cm (45¼in) diameter when blocked

PATTERN

▷ CENTRAL SECTION

Foundation ring: using 5.5mm hook and yarn A, ch5, ss to form ring

Round 1: ch4 (counts as first tr, ch1), [tr, ch1] 7 times into ring, ss into 3rd of starting ch4

Round 2: ss into ch-sp, s-tr, [tr, ch1] into same ch-sp, [2tr, ch1] into each ch-sp around, ss into top of s-tr

Round 3: s-tr, ch1, [3tr shell, ch1] into each ch-sp around, 2tr into last ch-sp, ss into top of s-tr

Round 4 (increase round): ss into ch-sp, s-tr, [tr, ch1, 2tr, ch1] into same ch-sp, [2tr, ch1] twice into each ch-sp around, ss into top of s-tr

Round 5: rep rnd 3

Round 6 (increase round): rep rnd 4

Round 7: s-tr, ch1, [2tr, ch1] into each ch-sp around, tr into last ch-sp, ss into top of s-tr

Round 8: ss into ch-sp, s-tr, [tr, ch1] into same ch-sp, [2tr, ch1] into each ch-sp around, ss into top of s-tr

Round 9: s-tr, 3tr shell into each ch-sp around, 2tr into last ch-sp, ss into top of s-tr, fasten off

Round 10: join yarn B between any 3tr shells of prev rnd, *ch3 (counts as first tr), 3tr shell into each sp between shells of prev rnd, 2tr into last sp*, fasten off invisibly

Round 11: join yarn A between any 3tr shells of prev rnd, rep rnd 10 from * to *, ss into 3rd of starting ch3

Round 12: ss into sp between shells of prev rnd, s-tr, [2tr, ch1] into same sp, [3tr shell, ch1] into each sp between shells of prev rnd, ss into top of s-tr, fasten off

Round 13: join yarn C in any ch-sp, ch4 (counts as first tr, ch1), [3tr shell, ch1] into each ch-sp around, 2tr into last ch-sp, fasten off invisibly

Round 14 (increase round): join yarn D in any ch-sp, *ch4 (counts as first tr, ch1), [2tr, ch1] twice into each ch-sp around, [2tr, ch1, tr] into last ch-sp*, fasten off invisibly

Round 15: join yarn A in any ch-sp, *ch4 (counts as first tr, ch1), [2tr, ch1] into each ch-sp around, tr into last ch-sp*, fasten off invisibly

Round 16: join yarn E in any ch-sp and rep rnd 15 from * to *, fasten off invisibly

▷ OUTER SECTION

Round 17: join yarn A in any ch-sp and rep rnd 15 from * to *, ss into 3rd of starting ch4

Round 18: rep rnd 8

Round 19: s-tr, ch1, [2tr, ch1] into each ch-sp around, tr into last ch-sp, ss into top of s-tr

Round 20: ss into ch-sp, s-tr, 2tr into same ch-sp, 3tr shell into each ch-sp around, ss into top of s-tr

Round 21: rep rnd 9, **do not fasten off**

Round 22: rep rnd 20

Round 23: rep rnd 9, **do not fasten off**

Round 24: rep rnd 12, fasten off

Round 25: join yarn C in any ch-sp, *ch4 (counts as first tr, ch1), [3tr shell, ch1] into each ch-sp around, 2tr into last ch-sp*, fasten off invisibly

Round 26: join yarn A in any ch-sp, rep rnd 25 from * to *, fasten off invisibly

Round 27: join yarn F in any ch-sp, *ch5 (counts as first tr, ch2), [3tr shell, ch2] into each ch-sp around, 2tr into last ch-sp*, fasten off invisibly

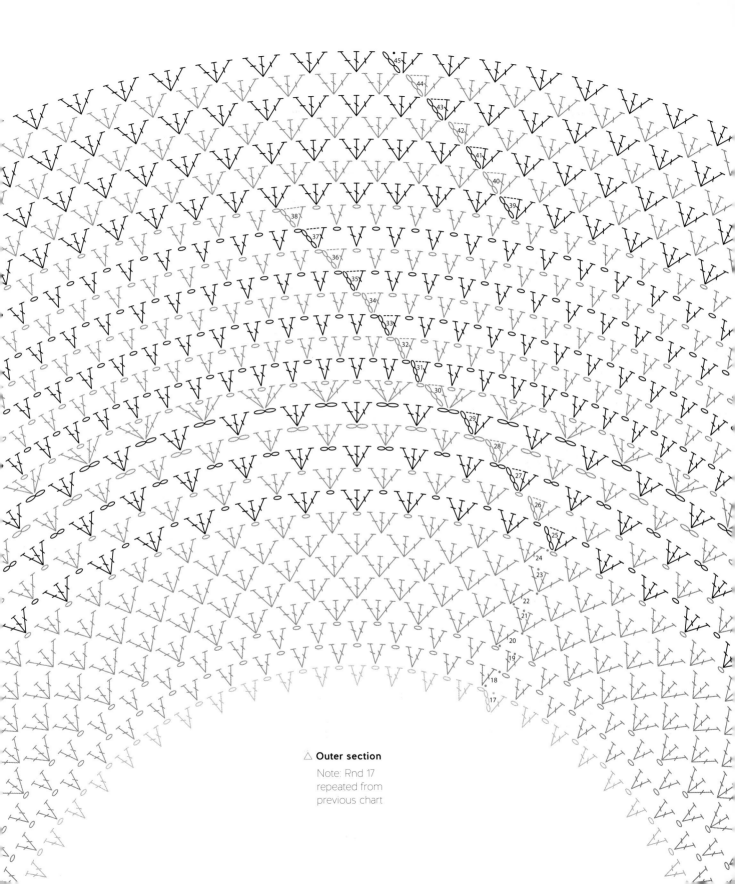

△ **Outer section**

Note: Rnd 17
repeated from
previous chart

Round 28: join yarn A in any ch-sp, rep rnd 27 from * to *, fasten off invisibly

Round 29: join yarn D in any ch-sp, rep rnd 27 from * to *, fasten off invisibly

Round 30 (increase round): join yarn A in any ch-sp, rep rnd 14 from * to *, fasten off invisibly

Round 31: join yarn G in any ch-sp, rep rnd 15 from * to *, fasten off invisibly

Round 32: join yarn E in any ch-sp, rep rnd 15 from * to *, fasten off invisibly

Round 33: rep rnd 31

Round 34: join yarn F in any ch-sp, rep rnd 15 from * to *, fasten off invisibly

Round 35: join yarn C in any ch-sp, rep rnd 15 from * to *, fasten off invisibly

Round 36: join yarn B in any ch-sp, rep rnd 15 from * to *, fasten off invisibly

Round 37: join yarn A in any ch-sp, rep rnd 15 from * to *, fasten off invisibly

Round 38: rep rnd 31

Round 39: join yarn A in any ch-sp, *ch3 (counts as first tr), 3tr shell into each ch-sp around, 2tr into last ch-sp*, fasten off invisibly

Round 40: join yarn D in any ch-sp, rep rnd 10 from * to *, fasten off invisibly

Round 41: join yarn A in any ch-sp, rep rnd 10 from * to *, fasten off invisibly

Round 42: join yarn F in any ch-sp, rep rnd 10 from * to *, fasten off invisibly

Round 43: rep rnd 41

Round 44: join yarn B in any ch-sp, rep rnd 10 from * to *, fasten off invisibly

Round 45: join yarn A in any ch-sp, rep rnd 10 from * to *, ss into 3rd of starting ch3

TIPS AND TRICKS

Large-scale circular designs can sometimes be tricky, even when you match the stated tension as closely as possible. Any minor cupping or rippling may be resolved with blocking. Address more pronounced cupping or rippling in the crochet process: after every few rounds lay out the work to see how it is progressing. If you have severe cupping, try omitting one or two rounds before the main increase round; for any severe rippling, try repeating the round before a main increase round once or twice. If you check your progress, making any necessary amendments as you go, your throw will lay flat.

▷ EDGING

Round 46: ss into sp between 3tr shells of prev rnd, s-tr, ch4, [tr, ch4] into each sp between shells of prev rnd, ss into top of s-tr

Round 47: ch1, ss into 2nd st of next ch4 sp, *8tr into next ch-sp, ss into next ch-sp* rep from * to * around, working last ss into same sp as first ss, fasten off and weave in loose ends

▷ BLOCKING

Using a press cloth, steam press on reverse with a hot iron to approx. 115cm (45¼in) diameter.

▽ **Edging**

Note: Rnd 45 repeated from previous chart

DAISY DOT
LAP BLANKET

We all need a little luxury in our lives, so when selecting yarns for our crochet projects, it pays to choose the best we can, especially when we invest so much of our time on our creations. For this pretty, colourful lap blanket I've chosen a high-quality, super soft, pure alpaca yarn that is surprisingly budget friendly. It is a joy to crochet with and will make the Daisy Dot Lap Blanket an heirloom piece that you will treasure for years to come.

△ Daisy motifs with
dot motif at centre

Tools and Materials

- Size 3.5mm (US E4) crochet hook
- 50g balls (167m/183yd) of Drops Alpaca, seven in shade 9020/Light Pearl Grey (yarn A), five in shade 1101/White (yarn B) and one each in shades 2915/Orange (yarn C), 2917/Turquoise (yarn D), 2923/Goldenrod (yarn E), 2921/Pink (yarn F), 3112/Dusty Pink (yarn G), 2916/Dark Lime (yarn H) and 5575/Navy Blue (yarn I)
- Yarn needle
- Scissors

Yarn Substitution

Any standard 4ply (fingering) or lightweight DK (sport) yarn can easily be substituted for the stated yarn; however, checking your tension carefully beforehand is strongly recommended.

Tension (Gauge)

7 rnds of circular motif worked in tr sts (12st inc each rnd) = 10cm (4in)

Each daisy motif should measure approx. 8.5cm (3¼in) diameter

Finished Size

Approx. 128cm (50¼in) long by 94cm (37in) wide

PATTERN

▷ DAISY MOTIF

Coloured Centre

Make 165: 24 each in yarns C, D, E and F and 23 each in yarns G, H and I.

Foundation ring: using yarn and 3.5mm hook create an adjustable ring

Round 1: ch4 (counts as first tr, ch1), [tr, ch1] 7 times into ring, close ring, ss into 3rd of starting ch4; fasten off

Flower Petals

Make 165 in yarn A.

Round 2: join yarn in any ch-sp, ch4 (counts as first tr, ch1), [3tr, ch1] into 7 ch-sps, 2tr into last ch-sp, ss into 3rd of starting ch4

Round 3: ch4 (counts as first tr, ch1), miss ch-sp of prev rnd, *†tr, 2tr inc†, tr, ch1* rep from * to * 7 times, rep from † to † once more, ss into 3rd of starting ch4

Round 4: ss into ch-sp, ch6 (counts as first tr, ch3), *†tr4tog, ch3†, tr into ch-sp, ch3* rep from * to * 7 times, rep from † to † once more, ss into 3rd of starting ch6, fasten off

Edging/Joining Rounds

Using the colour placement diagram as a guide, arrange the motifs in the correct colour order and work the final round to join the motifs as follows:

FIRST ROW:

Motif 1, round 5: join yarn B in any ch-sp before a tr4tog st of prev rnd, ch3 (counts as first tr), 4tr into each ch-sp around, 3tr into last ch-sp (64sts); fasten off invisibly

Motifs 2–11, round 5: join yarn B in any ch-sp, ch3 (counts as first tr), 4tr into next 12 ch-sps, jn into 17th edging st of first (or prev) motif, 4tr into next 3 ch-sps, 3tr into last ch-sp; fasten off invisibly

SECOND ROW:

Motif 12, round 5: join yarn B in any ch-sp, ch3 (counts as first tr), 4tr into next 8 ch-sps, jn into 2nd edging st of first motif, 4tr into next 7 ch-sps, 3tr into last ch-sp; fasten off invisibly

Motifs 13–22, round 5: join yarn B in any ch-sp, ch3 (counts as first tr), 4tr into next 8 ch-sps, jn into 2nd edging st of 2nd (or 3rd, 4th, etc.) motif of prev row, 4tr into next 4 ch-sps, jn into 17th edging st of first (or prev) motif in same row, 4tr into next 3 ch-sps, 3tr into last ch-sp; fasten off invisibly

REMAINING ROWS:

Join rows 3 to 15 as given for second row.

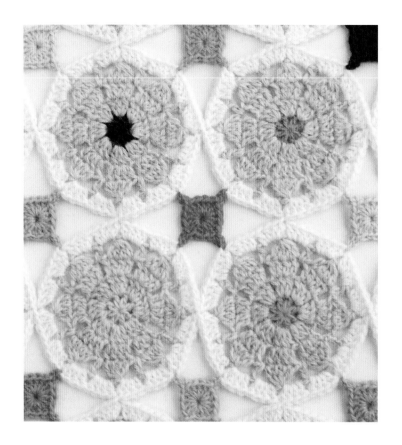

▷ DOT MOTIF

Make 140: 20 each in yarns C, D, E, F, G, H and I.

Each dot motif is crocheted between four daisy motifs, joining them as you go. Using the colour placement diagram as a guide, work each dot motif as follows:

Foundation ring: using yarn and 3.5mm hook ch5, ss to form ring

Round 1: ch3 (counts as first tr), 2tr, ch2, jn into 42nd edging st of top left motif, ch2, ss into top of prev tr st (as in a picot st), 4tr, ch2, jn into 58th edging st of bottom left motif, ch2, ss into top of prev tr st (as in a picot st), 4tr, ch2, jn into 26th edging st of top right motif, ch2, ss into top of prev tr st (as in a picot st), 2tr; fasten off invisibly and weave in loose ends

▷ BLOCKING

Using a press cloth, steam block on reverse with a hot iron to approx. 128cm (50¾in) long by 94cm (37in) wide.

 TIPS AND TRICKS

If you add the dot motifs as you go, you will find that the work is much easier to handle than if you were to add them at the end once all the daisy motifs have been joined together. So add the first row of dot motifs as soon as the first two rows of daisy motifs have been joined together, then alternate between adding a row of daisy motifs with a row of dot motifs.

COLOUR PLACEMENT

- ▶ Light Pearl Grey
- ▶ White
- ▶ Orange
- ▶ Turquoise
- ▶ Goldenrod
- ▶ Pink
- ▶ Dusty Pink
- ▶ Dark Lime
- ▶ Navy Blue

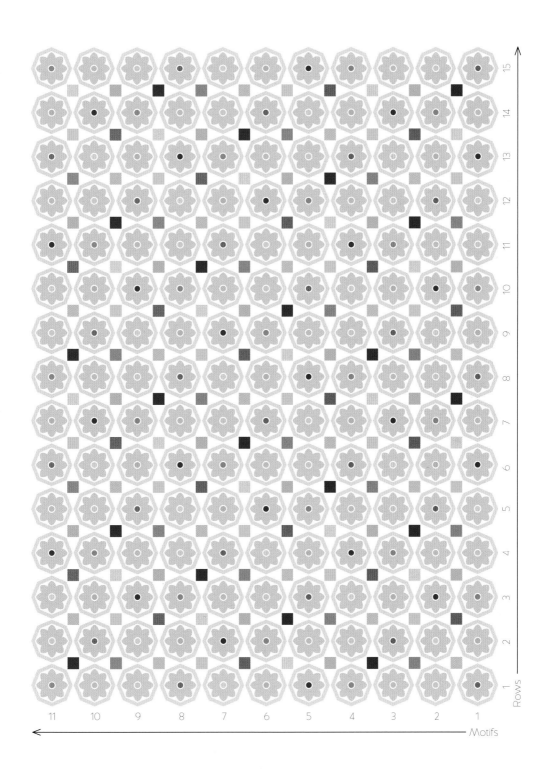

Rows

Motifs

15 14 13 12 11 10 9 8 7 6 5 4 3 2 1

11 10 9 8 7 6 5 4 3 2 1

GRANNY CHIC PINWHEEL BLANKET

The humble granny square is a crochet icon that has stood the test of time, providing many crocheters with endless hours of colourful crochet therapy. However, in the spirit of granny chic style, it is always exciting to find new ways to rejuvenate and refresh a classic, so here I've incorporated the granny square into a fabulously pretty pinwheel design. My Granny Chic Pinwheel Blanket is the perfect blend of retro and modern.

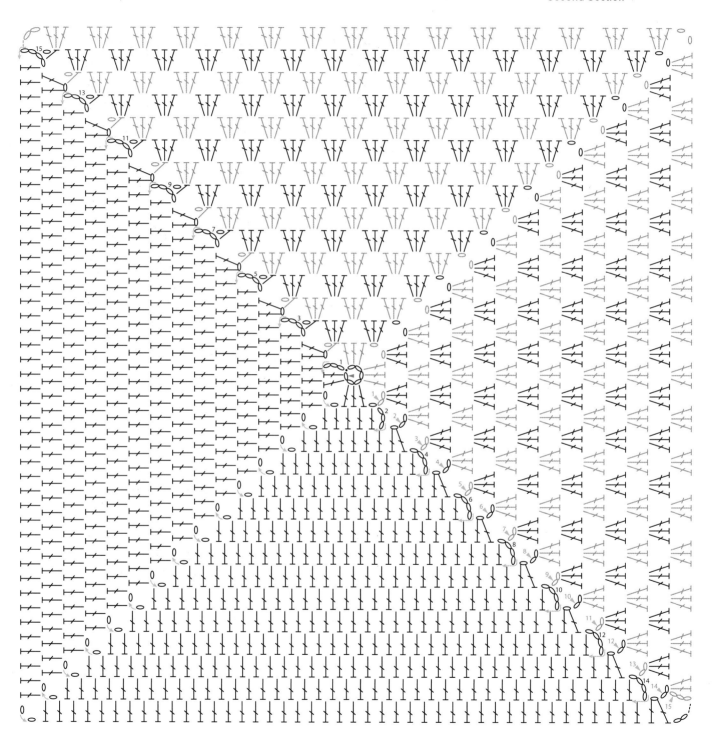

△ **First Section**

Tools and Materials

- Size 4.5mm (US 7) crochet hook
- 100g balls (200m/219yd) of Rowan Pure Wool Worsted, 16 in shade 101/Ivory (yarn A), two each in shades 112/Moonstone (yarn B), 132/Buttercup (yarn C) and 137/Oxygen (yarn D), and one each in shades 113/Pretty Pink (yarn E), 119/Magenta (yarn F), 131/Mustard (yarn G), 134/Seville (yarn H), 135/Papaya (yarn I), 140/Bottle (yarn J), 144/Mallard (yarn K) and 152/Oats (yarn L)
- Stitch holders (small safety pins or scrap yarn)
- Yarn needle
- Scissors

Yarn Substitution

Any standard DK (light worsted) weight yarn can easily be substituted for the stated yarn; however, checking your tension carefully beforehand is strongly recommended.

Tension (Gauge)

Each triangle square motif should measure 28cm (11¼in) square

5 rnds of granny square motif worked in tr sts = 10cm (4in)

Finished Size

Approx. 200cm (78¾in) long by 144cm (56¾in) wide

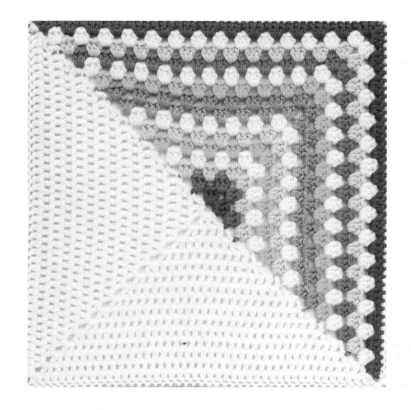

PATTERN

The triangle square motif is crocheted in two halves: the first section in one colour, where the work is turned at the end of each round; the second granny square section in multiple colours, where each round is worked individually in the same direction. It is then crocheted onto the first section and joined at the beginning and end of each round with slip stitches and half treble stitches. For step-by-step guidance on where to accurately work these stitches, see **Techniques**.

Triangle Square Motif – First Section

Make 35.

Foundation ring: using yarn A and 4.5mm hook, ch6, ss to form ring

Round 1 (RS): ch3 (counts as first tr), 2tr, ch2, 3tr, ch1, **turn**

Round 2: ch3 (counts as first tr), tr into 4th ch from hook, tr into 2 side sps (between tr sts of prev rnd), [2tr, ch2, 2tr] into corner ch-sp, tr into 2 side sps, f2tr inc into 3rd of ch3 of prev rnd, ch1, **turn**

Round 3: ch3 (counts as first tr), tr into 4th ch from hook, tr into 5 side sps, [2tr, ch2, 2tr] into corner ch-sp, tr into 5 side sps, f2tr inc into 3rd of ch3 of prev rnd, ch1, **turn**

Round 4: ch3 (counts as first tr), tr into 4th ch from hook, tr into 8 side sps, [2tr, ch2, 2tr] into corner ch-sp, tr into 8 side sps, f2tr inc into 3rd of ch3 of prev rnd, ch1, **turn**

Rounds 5–15: rnds 1–3 set the method for the simple single-colour part of the pinwheel, rep these rnds increasing the number of side sts by 3 in each new rnd; at the end of rnd 15 ch2, slip the working loop onto a stitch holder and cut a 15cm (6in) tail of yarn

Triangle Square Motif – Second Section

Make 35.

The colour placement in the second section of each triangle square motif is worked randomly using yarns A–L. However, one ball of yarn A and half a ball of yarn B should be kept aside to work the joining seams and edging.

Round 1: with RS facing, join yarn in ch st at the end of rnd 1 of first section, ch2, [3tr, ch2, 3tr] into foundation ring of first section, htr into base of f2tr inc of rnd 2 of first section, ch1, fasten off

Round 2: with RS facing, join yarn in base of f2tr inc at the end of rnd 3 of first section, ch2, 3tr shell into ch-sp, [3tr, ch2, 3tr] into corner ch-sp, 3tr shell into ch-sp,

htr into ch st the end of rnd 2 of first section, ch1, fasten off

Round 3: with RS facing, join yarn in ch st at the end of rnd 3 of first section, ch2, 3tr shell into ch-sp, 3tr shell into side sp, [3tr, ch2, 3tr] into corner ch-sp, 3tr shell into side sp, 3tr shell into ch-sp, htr into base of f2tr inc of rnd 4 of first section, ch1, fasten off

Round 4: with RS facing, join yarn in base of f2tr inc at the end of rnd 5 of first section, ch2, 3tr shell into ch-sp, 3tr shell into 2 side sps, [3tr, ch2, 3tr] into corner ch-sp, 3tr shell into 2 side sps, 3tr shell into ch-sp, htr into ch st the end of rnd 4 of first section, ch1, fasten off

Rounds 5–14: rnds 3 and 4 set the method for adding the granny square part of the pinwheel. Continue in this way, joining a new colour for each new rnd and increasing the number of 3tr shells along each side by 1 in each time

Round 15: join yarn in first ch-sp of prev rnd, ch3 (counts as first tr), 2tr into same sp, 13 x 3tr shell, [3tr, ch2, 3tr] into corner ch-sp, 14 x 3tr shell, ch2, fasten off invisibly to 3rd of starting ch3 of rnd 15 of first section

Finish Triangle Square Motif

Next: using yarn needle, pick up tail of yarn from end of first section and fasten off invisibly to 3rd of starting ch3 of rnd 15 of second section

Blocking Triangle Square Motifs

Steam block each triangle square motif to approx. 28cm (11¼in) square.

▷ MAKING UP

Joining Triangle Square Motifs

Arrange the triangle square motifs face up in a 5 x 7 grid, as shown in the photograph, to create a pinwheel design.

Using yarn A, join the motifs from the back working in rows of dc stitches horizontally then vertically. Crochet 1 dc into each corner ch-sp (ch-sp and side st where there is a colour change in the corner of the triangle square motif) and 1 dc into the top of each side st. When working the vertical joining rows, simply crochet over the top of the horizontal rows when you come to them.

Edging

Round 1: join yarn A in any corner ch-sp of blanket, ch3 (counts as first tr), *tr into top of each st and ch-sp of each triangle square motif along side of blanket, 5tr into corner ch-sp of blanket* rep from * to * to first corner of blanket, 4tr into corner ch-sp, fasten off invisibly

Round 2: join yarn B in first st before any 5tr corner sts of prev rnd, ch1, dc into same sp, *[dc, 2dc inc into next 3sts, dc] over next 5 corner sts, dc into each st to next corner* rep from * to * to end, fasten off invisibly

▷ BLOCKING

Using a press cloth, steam block seams and edging so that they lie flat.

BASIC STITCHES & TECHNIQUES

Note: UK [US]. See Pattern Abbreviations & Symbols for key.

⟳ Adjustable ring (or magic loop)

The adjustable ring method (or magic loop as it is also known) is used in motifs, such as squares and circles, that are worked in rounds. It is especially useful for creating a tight foundation ring that can be closed completely, unlike a chain stitch ring. It is also good for motifs that are worked outwards from a point, eliminating the unsightly knot of a slip knot loop from the beginning of the work to give a much neater finish.

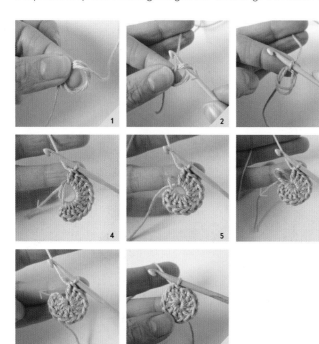

1: Holding tail of yarn securely, wrap the working yarn twice around the tip of your forefinger,

2: slip the ring off your finger and insert hook to pick up working yarn,

3: pull through to create a starting loop and chain 1 to secure; continue with first round of pattern as required.

4: To close the ring, pull on the tail of yarn to begin closing the first ring,

5: before the first ring is closed, pull on this ring to close the second ring tightly (take care not to pull the tail of yarn),

6: pull on the tail of yarn to tightly close the first ring,

7: complete the first round with a slip stitch or as required by the pattern.

8: Completed adjustable ring with first round of pattern.

Note: Remember to thoroughly weave in the tail of yarn to secure the adjustable ring.

⟳ ch

1: Make a slip knot loop and place on hook,

2: yarn over hook and pull through loop,

3: repeat step 2 as required.

• ss

 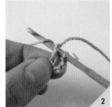 

1: Insert hook into work,

2: yarn over hook and pull loop through, and through first loop on hook.

3: Completed ss with foundation ring.

+ dc [sc]

1: Insert hook into work,

2: yarn over hook and pull loop through,

3: yarn over hook and pull through 2 loops.

┬ htr [hdc]

1: Yarn over hook and insert hook into next st in work,

2: yarn over hook and pull loop through,

3: yarn over hook and pull through 3 loops.

┬ tr [dc]

1: Work steps 1 and 2 of htr into next stitch,

2: yarn over hook and pull through 2 loops,

3: yarn over hook and pull through remaining 2 loops to complete the stitch.

dtr [tr]

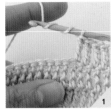 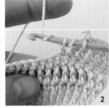 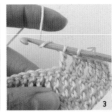

1: Yarn round hook twice and insert hook into work, yarn over hook and pull loop through,

2: yarn over hook and pull through 2 loops twice,

3: yarn over hook and pull through last 2 loops to complete the stitch.

INCREASING & DECREASING

2dc inc [2sc inc]

Work as given for dc twice into the same place.

2tr inc [2dc inc]

Work as given for tr twice into the same place.

3tr shell [dc shell]

Work as given for tr three times into the same place.

tr2tog [dc2tog]

1: Work steps 1 and 2 of tr stitch into next stitch,

2: rep step 1 into following st,

3: yarn over hook and pull through all loops on hook to complete the stitch, decreasing 2 tr stitches together.

tr3tog [dc3tog]

Work as given for tr2tog decreasing 3 tr stitches together

tr4tog [dc4tog]

Work as given for tr2tog decreasing 4 tr stitches together.

dtr2tog [tr2tog]

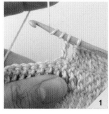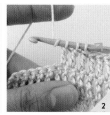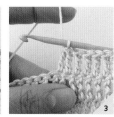

1: Work steps 1 and 2 of dtr stitch into next stitch,

2: rep step 1 into following st,

3: yarn over hook and pull through all loops on hook to complete the stitch.

DECORATIVE STITCHES

 3tr-cl [3dc-cl]

1: Work steps 1 to 3 of tr stitch into next stitch,

2: rep step 1 twice more into same place,

3: yarn over hook and pull through all loops on hook to complete the stitch.

 4tr-cl [4dc-cl]

Work as given for 3tr-cl repeating step 1, four times into same place.

 2dtr-cl [2tr-cl]

Work steps 1 and 2 of dtr twice into next stitch, yarn over hook and pull through all loops on hook to complete the stitch.

 3dtr-cl [3tr-cl]

Work steps 1 and 2 of dtr three times into next stitch, yarn over hook and pull through all loops on hook to complete the stitch.

5tr-fpcl [5dc-fpcl]

1: Yarn over hook and, from the front of work, insert hook from right to left under stitch in previous row,

2: yarn over hook and pull loop through,

3: yarn over hook and pull through 2 loops,

4: rep steps 1 to 3 four more times onto same stitch of prev row,

5: yarn over hook and pull through all loops on hook to complete the stitch.

6: Completed 5tr-fpcl.

pc

Each pattern that uses the popcorn stitch will include notes on the type of basic stitch used within it, the number of those stitches and whether it is finished with a chain stitch or not. These instructions demonstrate a 5 treble popcorn stitch finished with a chain stitch.

1: Work 5 treble stitches into same space, and slip working loop off hook,

2: insert hook into top of first treble stitch, from front to back, and place working loop on hook,

3: pull working loop through and pull tight, so that popcorn stitch 'pops' to the front of the work, chain 1.

sdc [ssc]

 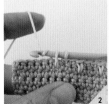 

1: From front of work insert hook into stitch 2 rows below, yarn over hook and pull loop through,

2: pull this loop long and to the height of the row currently working,

3: yarn over hook and pull through 2 loops on hook to complete the stitch.

bp-htr [bp-dc]

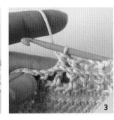

1: Yarn over hook and, from the back of the work, insert hook from right to left under stitch in previous row,

2: yarn over hook and pull loop through,

3: yarn over hook and pull through all loops on hook to complete the stitch.

SPECIAL STITCHES & TECHNIQUES

s-tr [s-dc] (no chains)

Starting treble stitches are best used when crochet is worked in rounds (eg square and circle motifs) in place of the familiar 'chain three' at the beginning of each round. They blend more neatly into the surrounding stitches, unlike the chain stitches, which can leave an unsightly starting line in the finished crochet piece.

1 and 1a: Pull working loop to the height of a treble stitch and hold in place with the tip of your forefinger, from right to left pass the hook behind the 2 threads of this loop,

2: yarn over and pull new loop to front of work so that there are 2 loops on the hook,

3: yarn over hook and pull through 2 loops.

4: Completed s-tr stitch.

5: To finish a round beginning with a s-tr, simply work a slip stitch into the top of the stitch and you are ready to work the next s-tr to begin the following round.

Invisible fasten off

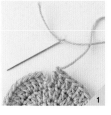   

1: At the end of a round cut a 15cm (6in) tail of yarn, pull working loop free through the top of the last stitch and thread onto a yarn needle,

2: insert the needle into the top of the first stitch of the round after the starting chain and pull the yarn through,

3 and 3a: from the top insert the needle down into the last stitch through the 2 back loops where the tail of yarn originally came from (see 3a),

4: pull the loop neatly closed and fasten off securely at the back of the starting chain.

5: Completed invisible fasten off.

− jn

Not technically a stitch as such, but a neat, quick and very effective method of joining individual motifs.

1: Slip working loop off hook,

2: insert hook into top of stitch of second motif and pick up working loop of first motif,

3: pull loop through stitch and continue in pattern.

+ jdc [jsc]

This joining stitch is used in the Filet Daisy Potholder pattern to line up the open meshwork of the design and maintain the filet effect in the finished potholder.

  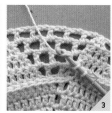

1: With two crochet panels laid back to back, insert hook under corresponding chain stitches of second motif,

2: yarn over and pull loop through,

3: yarn over and pull through 2 loops to complete the dc stitch, and continue in pattern.

⬭ pf

 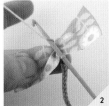 

1: Take a fabric snippet and gather it at the centre,

2: place the gathered fabric between the hook and working yarn,

3: tightly chain 1 to hold the fabric in place.

⊻ f2tr inc [f2dc inc]

Foundation stitches are usually used to work foundation rows for large flat crochet pieces (blankets, etc.) to avoid the tedious task of trying to accurately count chain stitches! However in this book they are used as a method of increasing in the triangle square motifs used in the pinwheel patterns. These instructions demonstrate how to increase at the end of a row.

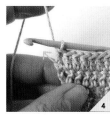 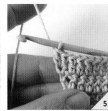

1: Yarn over hook and insert hook into third of starting ch3 of previous row, yarn over hook and pull loop through,

2: yarn over hook and pull through 1 loop to create foundation chain,

3: yarn over hook and continue to complete tr stitch,

4: work a second tr into the same foundation chain.

5: Completed f2tr inc.

Triangle square for pinwheel patchwork + log cabin cushion covers

Joining stitches second section

Beginning round 1

Make a slip knot loop and place on your index finger.

1: With right side of first section of triangle square facing, insert hook into chain st at end of rnd 1 going under 2 threads of the stitch,

2: place slip knot loop on hook and pull through,

3: chain 1 and continue in pattern.

  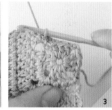

End round 1

1: Insert hook into foundation chain of f2tr inc, making sure to go under 2 threads as indicated,

2: yarn over hook and work a slip stitch.

3: Round 1 completed.

Beginning round 2

1: Chain 2 and yarn over hook, insert hook into chain stitch at the end of rnd 2 of first section as indicated,

2: yarn over hook and pull loop through,

3: yarn over hook and pull through all loops to complete half treble stitch, turn and continue in pattern.

End round 2 and following rounds

1: As before, insert hook into foundation chain of f2tr inc going under 2 threads,

2: yarn over hook and work a slip stitch.

3: To complete a full triangle square motif, continue for as many rounds as required beginning and ending each round as given for rnd two.

Triangle square for granny chic pinwheel blanket

Joining stitches for second section

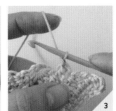

Beginning round 1

Make a slip knot loop and place on your index finger.

1: With right side of first section of triangle square facing, insert hook into chain st at end of rnd 1 going under 2 threads of stitch,

2: place slip knot loop on hook and pull through,

3: chain 1 and continue in pattern.

End round 1

1: Yarn over hook and insert hook into foundation chain of f2tr inc, making sure to go under 2 threads as indicated,

2: yarn over and pull loop through,

3: yarn over and continue to complete half treble stitch,

4: yarn over hook and chain 1,

5: cut a 15cm (6in) tail of yarn, pull last loop free and pull thread tight to secure the fasten off.

6: Completed round 1.

Beginning round 2

Work as given for beg of rnd 1 inserting hook into foundation chain of f2tr inc, making sure to go under 2 threads as indicated.

End round 2 and following rounds

Work as given for end of rnd 1 working half treble stitch into chain stitch at end of rnd 2 of first section. Continue for as many rounds as required for a full triangle square motif, working odd numbered rounds as rnd 1, and even numbered rounds as rnd 2.

ABOUT THE AUTHOR

Emma Lamb is a British crochet designer and blogger living in the beautiful city of Edinburgh, Scotland. She lives with her Man and dog, Spanner the English Cocker Spaniel, and spends her days dreaming in colourful crochet. With every new design Emma strives to rejuvenate the joy and appreciation for this traditional craft with pieces that easily fit into our everyday lives, with an eye for detail and quality her designs are practical but beautiful works of art. Through her crochet Emma explores fresh and playful combinations of colour, pattern and texture with a nod to 'retro' styles and draws inspiration from the Scandinavian aesthetic, mid-century design and her everyday life.

ACKNOWLEDGMENTS

To my little family Mark & Spanner, and of course my Mam & Dad, your support has been invaluable!

Very special thanks to my new friends Anna and Jason for their vision, passion and dedication to this project and for being so wonderful and easy to work with.

Also to Kang for his exceptional charting skills and enthusiasm. These guys are the best and I couldn't have made this book without them!

Thank you also to the hardworking team at David & Charles for making this book a reality.

To Yasmina and her beautiful family, a heartfelt thank you for sharing your lovely home with us.

To my yarn-loving friends Debbie, Enrico, Linda, Kate and Lindsay – I thank you for sharing your passion for beautiful yarns with the world!

Last but by no means least, a huge, huge thank you to everyone who has supported my crochet work, blog and colourful Pinterest addiction over the years; without you this book would have not been possible. I hope you all enjoy it as much as I have enjoyed creating it for you!?

Book babies: Alice Bea Gardner.

SUPPLIERS

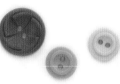

▷ SKEIN QUEEN
www.skeinqueenyarns.co.uk
Lustrous hand-dyed yarn in one-of-a-kind colour ways.

▷ GOMITOLI'S
www.gomitolis.it
Luxury Italian yarns, including cashmere, merino wool and camel hair.

▷ YARN STORIES
www.yarnstories.etsy.com
Lithuanian linen yarn available in four different thicknesses with a huge choice of colours.

▷ PAPERPHINE
www.shop.paperphine.com
Finest paper yarns and paper twines.

▷ ROWAN
www.knitrowan.com
Luxurious hand-knitting yarns featuring premium fibres, all in a diversely rich and authentically natural colour palette.

▷ LOOP
www.loopknitting.com
A leading UK yarn shop, stocking gorgeous knitting and crochet patterns as well as the yummiest selection of yarns sourced from all over the world, both in their London shop and online.

▷ DMC
www.dmccreative.co.uk
Well known as a supplier of quality cotton yarns in a variety of weights and comprehensive colour palettes.

▷ BLUE SKY ALPACAS
www.blueskyalpacas.com
Exclusive yarns in contemporary and classic colours for hand knits and crochet. The collection includes fine quality alpaca, wool, silk and organic cotton in unique blends.

▷ DROPS
www.garnstudio.com
A wide range of high quality yet affordable natural fibre and blended yarns in extensive colour palettes.

▷ JOHN LEWIS
www.johnlewis.com
A leading UK department store with fantastic haberdashery departments, stocking crochet accessories and a wide range of Rowan yarns amongst others.

▷ LOVE KNITTING
www.loveknitting.com
Extensive range of crochet accessories and commercial yarns, including both British and American brands such as Blue Sky Alpacas and Drops.

▷ DERAMORES
www.deramores.com
Extensive range of crochet accessories and commercial yarns, including DMC cottons.

▷ FRED ALDOUS
www.fredaldous.co.uk
Extensive range of craft and haberdashery supplies, including crochet notions and metal lampshade rings.

▷ THE FEATHER COMPANY
www.thefeathercompany.com
Quality cushions, pillows, bolsters, duvets and feather wrapped foam cushions, all hand-filled using only the best quality natural fillings.

▷ FOLKSY
www.folksy.com
Notions, handmade crochet supplies and accessories, hand dyed and handspun yarns from independent businesses across the United Kingdom.

▷ ETSY
www.etsy.com
A great resource for a wide range of craft suppliers of both new and vintage notions, crochet accessories and independent yarn dyers and spinners worldwide.

INDEX

A DAVID & CHARLES BOOK
© F&W Media International, Ltd 2015

David & Charles is an imprint of
F&W Media International, Ltd., Brunel House,
Forde Close, Newton Abbot, TQ12 4PU, UK

F&W Media International, Ltd is a subsidiary
of F+W Media, Inc., 10151 Carver Road,
Suite #200, Blue Ash, OH 45242, USA

Text and Designs © Emma Lamb 2015
Layout and Photography
© F&W Media International, Ltd 2015,
except pages 130 -139 © Emma Lamb 2015

First published in the UK and USA in 2015

A catalogue record for this book is
available from the British Library.

ISBN-13: 978-1-4463-0485-3 paperback
ISBN-10: 1-4463-0485-X paperback

ISBN-13: 978-1-4463-6750-6 PDF
ISBN-10: 1-4463-6750-9 PDF

ISBN-13: 978-1-4463-6751-3 EPUB
ISBN-10: 1-4463-6751-7 EPUB

Printed in China by RR Donnelley for:
F&W Media International, Ltd
Brunel House, Forde Close,
Newton Abbot, TQ12 4PU, UK

10 9 8 7 6 5 4 3 2 1

Acquisitions Editor: Sarah Callard
Managing Editor: Honor Head
Project Editors: Jane Trollope, Emma Gardner
Art Editor: Anna Fazakerley
Designer: Lorraine Inglis
Photographer: Jason Jenkins
Stylist: Emma Lamb
Production Controller: Beverley Richardson

F+W Media publishes high quality books
on a wide range of subjects. For more great
book ideas visit: www.stitchcraftcreate.co.uk

Layout of the digital edition of this
book may vary depending on reader
hardware and display settings.